CARNEGIE LIBRARY OF PITTSBURGH

Social Sciences Department

Hannah's Daughters: Six Generations of an American Family, 1876–1976

All the Right Enemies: The Life and Murder of Carlo Tresca

HOW I CAME INTO MY INHERITANCE

HOW I CAME INTO

MY INHERITANCE

and Other True Stories

DOROTHY GALLAGHER

RANDOM HOUSE

NEW YORK

RANDOM HOUSE and colophon are registered trademarks of
Random House, Inc.

Portions of this book were originally published in *The New York
Times Book Review, Raritan*, and *Areté* (England)

Library of Congress Cataloging-in-Publication Data
Gallagher, Dorothy.
How I came into my inheritance : and other true stories / Dorothy Gallagher.
p.   cm.
ISBN 0-375-50346-3 (acid-free paper)—
ISBN 0-375-70750-6 (pbk. : acid-free paper)
1. Gallagher, Dorothy. 2. New York (N.Y.)—Biography. I. Title.
CT275.G248 A3 2001   974.7'1043'092—dc21
[B]   00-041471

Random House website address: www.atrandom.com
Printed in the United States of America on acid-free paper
2 4 6 8 9 7 5 3
First Edition

Book design by J. K. Lambert

Memory at last has what it sought.

My mother has been found, my father glimpsed.

I dreamed up for them a table, two chairs.

They sat down . . .

—Wisława Szymborska

CONTENTS

HOW I CAME INTO MY INHERITANCE

HOW I CAME INTO

MY INHERITANCE

—

After my mother broke her hip, I put her in a nursing home.

"You want to put me here?" she said.

The woman was certified senile, but she still knew how to push my buttons. Not that she didn't have reason to worry; had I listened when she'd begged me "Darling, please, please don't do anything to hurt Daddy. It will kill him . . ."?

I swear, what I did, it wasn't just for the money.

You know that tone people take about old age? The stuff about dignity and wisdom and how old people (pardon me for saying *old*) should be allowed to make their own decisions. Allowed! My father treated nicely reasoned arguments like mosquitoes. As for dignity, let's pass over the question of bodily wastes for the moment; let's suppose that the chronologically challenged father of one such pious person decided to torture and starve his or her chronologically challenged mother. ("So she falls! She'll lie there till she gets up! . . . What does she need orange juice for? If she's thirsty she'll drink water!") And not only that, but also gives away practically all that person's inheritance to a crook. Do you think you might see any revisionism in attitude then?

Until the day I took him to court and the judge laid down the law, nobody, but nobody, interfered with my father. I mean, he was awesome. For instance, he owned this slum building. It was filled with some characters you wouldn't want to meet in broad daylight on a busy street. The tenants didn't pay rent, welfare paid the rent. But welfare didn't pay *exactly* as much as my father was legally entitled to. So every month, even when he was up in his late eighties, he'd get in his car and drive over to that building, haul himself up the stairs, bang his cane on every door, and demand his five or ten dollars. He got it. Nobody laid a finger on him. Nobody even slammed the door in his face. And the only way you could tell he might be even a little bit nervous was that he left his motor running. And the *car* was never stolen!

It wasn't easy to tell when my father began to lose his marbles, because he'd always been such a headstrong summabitch, as he called everyone who had a slightly different idea. But the winter he was ninety he took out the water heater. That was a clue. I went up there one day—they lived about sixty miles upstate in this house they'd lived in forever. Now, the house should have been my first clue. I knew that house. I grew up there. If ever there was a homemade house, that was it. My father built it all around us. First we were living in two rooms, then three; nine by the time he got finished, the rooms all stuck on in unexpected places, connected by closets you walked through to get to other rooms, short dark corridors and twisting staircases. He never got tired of making new rooms. When I was a kid I thought he had made the world. Like once, we needed a shovel for the woodstove. My father took a metal ice tray, cut off one end, rounded it, put a hole in the other end, and stuck a bit of pipe in. *Voilà!* I idolized that man.

And now the house was a wreck: jury-rigged electrical cords you tripped over, water dripping from the roof, buckets on the floor, smells of accumulated filth. I'd piss in my pants before I'd go into the bathroom. But the thing is, I still believed in my father; he'd always taken care of everything. So when I'd say, "Daddy, there's a leak over Mama's bed. Let me find someone to fix the roof," and he'd say, "Don't you do anything, I'll take care of it," I'd think, Okay, I guess he knows what he's doing.

Or I might say, "I'll get somebody to clean the house."

"It's clean! Mama cleans!"

So I say, "Mama, when did you clean the house?" She says, dementedly, "You saw, I just swept out. You know it doesn't get so dirty in the country."

I say, "But it smells bad," and my father says, "It doesn't smell!" I'd think: He seems sure. I guess it's not so bad. And everything happened so gradually.

Anyway, I'd go up to see them once a week or so, and this one time I find my father is hacking up pieces of scrap wood.

"Daddy," I say. "What are you doing?"

He cackles. *Hee hee hee.* I'm not making fun of him. That's the way he sounds. "I took out the water heater," he says, and he's rubbing his hands together in glee. "I'm putting in a wood-fired heater."

"Why, Daddy?"

"We'll heat with wood. It's cheaper."

"But, *Daddy!*" I say, and that's all I say. I don't mention that the outside stairs to the basement are icy in winter. I don't remind him that he's ninety years old and he can hardly get up and down the stairs in good weather. I don't say that my mother's hands will crack and bleed doing dishes in cold water, or that bathing, which is a once-a-month affair at best now, will occur never. I say, "But, *Daddy!*" because I know if I say any more, he'll say, "It's not your *business!*" And I'd think: Well, I guess it's not my business. And the truth is I'm still scared of him.

My father is really something. Everybody says so: "That Izzy. He's really something." They mean he's a force of nature; he takes his course no matter what. If he doesn't know it, it's not worth knowing; if it's not done his way, it's done wrong; what he doesn't like reading isn't worth the paper. One time I gave him a book by this Nobel Prize winner. "Tell him to get another trade!" my father said, no discussion.

About a year after he took out the water heater, he was in the hospital for a month. How he made it out alive, I'll never know. "Ninety-one," the nurses said. "God bless him." He comes home with tubes sticking out of everything. A tube out of you-know-where for his urine, a tube from his gallbladder. I get a nurse to take care of him. Two days later he calls me up: "Get her out of here! Get her out!" So I tell the nurse she'd better leave and I run up on the train to empty his pee bag and his bile bag. I got his *bile* on my *hands!*

My mother is no help, of course. She can hardly keep on her own feet. She's falling down every five minutes. I say, "Daddy, we have to have help. You don't want a nurse, okay. But for Mama. She falls." I think maybe I'll get around him that way.

"She doesn't fall!"

"I don't fall," my mother says. "When do I fall?"

"Mama! I just picked you up! Daddy, you saw! I just picked her up."

"So *I'll* pick her up."

We're sitting on the porch. My mother gets up. She thinks she's going to the kitchen to make lunch. She hasn't cooked anything for two years. *I* bring the food. She takes two steps, and falls down. My father says, "Watch!" He inches his chair closer to her and sticks out his cane.

"Belle! Grab the cane!"

The woman doesn't know what's going on, she only knows the master of the universe has spoken. She grabs the cane. "Get up!" he orders, and she tries to haul herself up. It takes about five minutes, with him desperately trying to hold the cane steady against her weight without falling out of his chair.

She's up! My father looks triumphant: "See!"

Right away she falls down again. This time he pretends he doesn't notice. He thinks he can get away with it because, on top of everything else, he's just about blind.

By now I'm really frantic. What am I supposed to do about this situation? I go to see some social-service people: Look, I say, my father's blind, he's been in the hospital three times with congestive heart failure and kidney failure, my mother's in really bad shape. I'm rushing up there every five minutes because there's another crisis, my father's a regular Collier brother, he's got plenty of money but he won't spend money for food, I got Meals-on-Wheels to come and he starts waving his cane around and yelling at them to get off his property, he won't have a nurse or even someone to clean up, he fires everybody I hire, they have no hot water, he keeps the thermostat below sixty in winter. If they die there'll be a headline in the paper: STARVING OLD COUPLE EATEN BY RATS: MILLION DOLLARS FOUND IN MATTRESS.

I don't know how many social-service types I told this story to. And in case they thought I was exaggerating, I had documentary evidence.

This house is very dangerous to work in. The man is a very bad man I think he's mad. When he don't want you around he say you steals his money. Before you working here ask around the neighborhood and everyone will say it's the truth. The woman is very nice and quite but him? It's the worst human being I've ever come across. Be careful and think first before you accept the job. His wife is very sick. She suffers with a fainting spell. When you getting this job he don't tell you this. He also is suffering from some disease. The food you have to cook turns you off, its like YAK. *His daughter lives in the city. She's a very nice person but he treats her bad.*

I don't know which of the aides my father fired wrote this note. Not the one who refused to masturbate him, or she would have mentioned it. But what did I get from the helping professions? I got a lot of Tsk tsk, really nothing we can do if your father refuses help, he has rights.

"What about my mother's rights?" I ask.

"I don't suppose you could move in yourself, dear?"

Probably you're wondering the same thing. Why don't I just move in with them? It's not that I didn't think about it. I thought about it every day. "If you're so worried about Mama, *you* take care of her!" my father once yelled at me. And it was getting so I was up there every other day, it was getting so I had no life but them, thought of nothing but them. But I couldn't move in. Could not. Okay, would not.

That's what this shrink I went to said. She said it was my choice. She said maybe I wanted my father to yell Uncle (I'm paraphrasing here), to say, Okay, kid, you were right, I was wrong, take over. Maybe so. But the way it felt to me was I *had* to go home every night. I *had* to take a breath that didn't smell of rot. I *had* to sleep in my own bed. If it had been just my mother, if I had known everything that was going on . . .

When I say "everything that was going on," I'm talking about the million dollars I thought was in the mattress. There wasn't any money in the mattress. My father, who, when I *plead* with him to get some help in the house, wails, "All my little savings will be gone!" had taken his hard-earned money, saved from a lifetime of work parking cars and pumping gas, not to mention extreme parsimony, and was giving it to some guy who promised to triple it.

By parsimony, I mean that when I was a kid this is how I learned to make a phone call: First you went to the telephone booth at the corner candy store. You dialed the operator for free, told her you'd been connected with a wrong number. In those innocent days the operator would return a nickel she believed to be your nickel and then connect you with the number you wanted. That's how my mother did it, that's how I did it, and that's one way the nickels added up.

The guy who was getting my father to give him his money

was some kind of genius. I don't mean that he's intelligent or educated or well-read or anything. He's a genius in his speciality, which happens to be getting money out of people. I'll tell you what he reminds me of—one of those guys who marries women in every state, gets them to turn over all their money to him, and then disappears. Finally one of the women tracks him down. Instead of being arrested, he goes on *Geraldo!* Six women appear on the show with him and say they don't care what he did, they won't press charges, all they want is to have him back because each of them *knows* that *she's* the one he really loves.

Roy, that's his name. I start asking around and I hear a few things. So I mention them. "Daddy," I say. "Want to guess what I heard about Roy?"

"He was just a kid," my father says. "Got into a little trouble." He seems as proud of the guy as if he'd learned his ways at my father's knee.

"Daddy," I say. "I saw the guy's bankruptcy petition. He owes almost a million dollars. A quarter of that is *yours!*"

"That's not *your* business," my father says. "It's *my* business. It's *business*. These things happen in business."

Anyway, the way I first learned about Roy is that once a month my father and I sit down at the kitchen table. Under the light from one fluorescent bulb, which is all he allows in the ceiling fixture, we go over his bank statement. I call out every check. He tries to remember what it was for. Then, if he *can* remember, I check it off on the statement. So every month I'm seeing these checks, written in a strange hand-writing but signed by my father's trembling hand at an extreme distance from the signature line. Checks are made out to building-supply companies, to lighting contractors, like that. And many of them are made out to this guy Roy. It's all adding up to a lot of money.

Finally I say: "Daddy. Who's this Roy?"

"We're in business!" he says.

"Oh gosh, you're in business, Daddy!" I do my best to sound delighted. How many ninety-three-year-old fathers choose this method of putting their affairs in order for their loved ones?

"What kind of business?"

"You wouldn't understand!"

"Daddy," I say, trying flattery. "Everybody says I got my brains from you. I *would* understand." Many wouldn't.

"We're putting up a development."

"Houses?"

"Twelve houses. Modulars. Roy's building the model."

"No kidding? He's your partner?"

"We have an arrangement."

"So when will these houses be finished?"

"A few years."

Don't think I don't realize that I'm faced with an ethical problem. This guy was a shark, that was clear enough. "Him!" said the local lawyers and businesspeople; everyone knew a story. But Roy understood certain things about my father. For instance, the greed at the heart of his parsimony, the same greed for life that makes old men hunch deep over their plates and shovel in the food. Roy flattered him; my father blushed like a girl when Roy praised his shrewdness. Roy promised he'd live forever and told him stories of ninety-nine-year-olds who ran the marathon. Roy promised him fabulous profits from their "development" that would materialize years in the future—years in my father's future. So what right did I have to interfere with my father's raison d'être? Or, as Roy says to me later on, when I *beg* him to use his influence to get yet another nurse's aide into the house, "A man's got a right to live the way a man wantsta live."

Summabitch, as my father would say.

At last I meet Roy. One day I go to the house, dragging bags of cooked food as usual. I always stop at the top of a small rise just before I get there. Standing on that hilltop, I can see my mother and father on the porch. What I actually see is a heap of rags bunched up on the mattress of the porch swing. That's my mother. My father is sitting on his wood-slatted metal chair, sort of rocking back and forth. Usually his radio is blaring Howard Stern or Bob Grant so loud I can hear it fifty yards away, but not today. Today I see he's talking to someone. Or rather, someone seems to be talking to him. Kneeling down in front of him in fact. Leaning toward him. Like he's begging or something. What is *this?*

"This is Roy," my father says.

Roy gets up off his knees when he sees me. He's not the least bit embarrassed. We take a good look at each other. I see a guy maybe in his late thirties, dark hair. He's not so tall, sort of stooped and round-shouldered, and he's got a little paunch. He sticks out his hand shyly and gives me a little smile, the kind where the teeth don't show. I can picture his smarmy face on a poster with the words WANTED and RE-WARD written above and below his photograph. That's what *I* see. What does he see? The fly in the ointment, no doubt.

"Your dad and I have a special relationship," he says. My father nods. "He's more like a dad to me than my own dad." My father beams. Then Roy remembers I have a "mom," too. He glances at the heap of rags on the swing and says, "And your mom, too."

"Mama," I say after Roy has taken my father to the "development" site. "Was Roy on his knees?"

"Yes," she says, very calmly.

"What was he doing?" I ask. I had no hope that anything had penetrated the fog of her stroke-damaged brain.

"You know. He wants money from Daddy. That one, what's his name? He's always asking Daddy for money." And then she says, asking my very own question, "Will there be anything left for us?"

"Daddy," I say to him soon after. "How do you feel about Roy?"

This is the kind of thing a woman asks a man she thinks has been cheating on her. There's no good news.

"Roy! He's like a son to me. He does more for me than a son would!" my father says to me.

I hear myself plead, "What about me, Daddy?" and before I can stop myself I'm reciting a list of my lifetime of devoted attentions.

"That's only natural," my father says. And then he looks straight at me with his bleary eyes. "Roy's got nothing to do with you! You want my money? You think *you* should have my money? It's *my* money. I'll do what I want with my money!"

So. Our lives had come down to this. Yes, I thought I should have his money. I thought it was only natural.

"Mama," I said. "I have to do something to stop Daddy from giving Roy all his money."

"Darling," she said. "Please, please don't do anything to hurt Daddy. It will kill him." A minute later she said, "It will kill me too."

I weighed their lives and mine, and I got a lawyer. Roy got my father a lawyer. My father's lawyer made a pretty good case for him; after all, he wasn't senile, just desperate to go on living. But the judge took one look at my ancient father, unable to stand in court, dressed in his filthy rags, and he made me my father's conservator. My father couldn't believe it. The look he gave me! *Bitter hatred.*

So what? Wasn't I *his* daughter?

"Mama," I said when we left the courthouse. "Do you understand what happened?"

"What did you do, darling?" she said. She put her hands over her face. *"Oh that I should live to see you and Daddy quarrel."*

Two weeks after the court ruling, my father was in the hospital. I went to the hospital every day. I had to. Roy was in a panic. All his plans were going down the tubes. Too bad I couldn't be in two places at once, because while I was at the hospital, Roy went to the house and took all the papers that showed how much money he owed my father. And then late one night he showed up at the hospital with a lawyer. They had a new will for my father to sign. I stopped them at the door.

"Daddy," I said. "Roy is here. Do you want to see him?"

I had to lean down, close to his mouth. He whispered, "Yes."

"He doesn't want to see you," I said to Roy.

"I don't believe you," Roy said. "Bitch," he said.

The lawyer said, "You have no right to stop us," but I stood in the doorway until they left. *Wasn't* I my father's daughter.

That night my father breathed his last. I sat in a chair next to his bed. I knew he was dying. The nurse said, "Shall I call the doctor?" I said, "No." I talked to my father. I urged him on. "It's okay, Daddy," I said. "Let go. Let go. It's been hard." I *wanted* to say "I love you, Daddy"; it came out "Mama loves you."

My mother let out such a cry when I told her. *"I'm all alone."* "You have me, Mama," I said. "Yes," she said. "That's everything." But when it came down to it, she was right.

Not long after my father died, my mother got out of bed in the middle of the night. She fell; her hip broke. In the hospital, coming out of the anesthesia, wild-eyed and flailing, she called *me* Mama. After that I had to put her in the nursing home.

The weeks passed. Every time I'd go to see her, she'd ask,

"When will we go home?" She was crazy with anxiety.

"Daddy will worry," she'd say. "Oh, Daddy died? . . . I had an operation? It's a good thing Daddy's not here to be asking questions. He'd say, 'What did she need it for? How can we afford it?' . . . You think Daddy misses me? . . . So when will we go home?"

"Soon, Mama."

"How will we get there? Daddy has the car."

"We'll take a taxi, Mama."

"You always were a spender," she said.

Those promises I made to her: Sure, Daddy misses you, we'll go home soon, I'll see you tomorrow, you're not alone. Mama. I didn't think she'd remember from one minute to the next. But now I think she did remember. I think she figured out that there was no Daddy, she'd never go home, I wouldn't come tomorrow, she'd die among strangers. Early one snowy winter morning, almost exactly nine months after my father, she died. Among strangers.

In my mother's room at the nursing home I'd hung a picture that was taken just after I was born. I'm lying on a tiny cot surrounded by a cage of screening my father made to protect his baby daughter from insects. Our house is still a cottage. The lawn looks like a wild meadow. My mother leans over the cot, and oh god, what a fiercely tender gaze she gives me! My father, slightly out of focus, is sitting on a porch chair behind her, smiling at the scene. In the foreground is the trunk of the big old elm where my father built a swing for me.

Never mind that. I was telling you how I came into my inheritance.

NO ONE IN MY FAMILY

HAS EVER DIED OF LOVE

—

No one in my family has ever died of love.
What happened, happened, but nothing
myth-inspiring.

—Wisława Szymborska

I put my mother's ashes on the floor of the closet, right next to my shoes. I left them there from December until March. In March, a year after my father's death, I bestirred myself. I called the funeral parlor where I had abandoned (*not* too strong a word) his ashes. I wondered how long they kept uncollected cremains. Yes. Cremains. My father's cremains were still on the shelf, so I collected them, and one day in early spring I took a trip up to the house with my cousins and two boxes of cremains.

I'd found a buyer for the house, but it was still empty. In a few months the new owners will gut the place: Walls will come down as though they hadn't been inevitable, new rooms will erase the old ones, the Formica paneling, meant to resemble ash wood, will be junked, the ancient linoleum will be ripped up, light will pour in through new skylights, a deck will be built, God help us.

On the day I saw those wonders I had to knock on the door, but this day my key still worked. We walked through the dark, dismal rooms. Except for the sour smell of decay, everything was gone: clothes, furniture, books—none of it good enough for the Salvation Army—had been thrown into a dumpster by men wearing gloves and surgical masks. Here, under the kitchen windows, was where the table stood, covered with its stained plastic cloth; here, against the wall in the small room next to the kitchen (where I had spent my first year), the ancient pullout couch where my father, with no breath to climb the twisting, narrow stairs, spent his last year; down the narrow hallway, the bathroom. I thought I could still see smears of feces on the walls. And on the other side of the bathroom wall, my mother's bed had stood. Two months a widow and she got up at five o'clock one May morning, fell, broke her hip. That was the beginning of the end.

———

I was at the age to notice things. One thing I noticed was that when men came home in the evening, they kissed their wives. In the summertime, when fathers were away in the city all week, they kissed them longer.

"Why don't you and Daddy kiss?" I asked my mother.

"The kid wants to know why we don't kiss," my mother must have said.

"She wants a kiss, we'll kiss," my father must have said, because the next weekend they kissed, conspicuously, four eyes slipping sideways to see if I was noticing.

Oh, the falseness! Did they take me for a fool?

But I wasn't drawing any hard-and-fast conclusions. Wasn't my very existence proof of their love? And there was other evidence too. For instance, that snapshot of them taken before I was born, where they're standing in a meadow, young and darkly sexy, with their arms around each other's shoulders. And then there was the story of how she had left him and run away to Canada (she was always cagey about the reason; other women? callous treatment?) and he went all the way up to Quebec to bring her back. That was a good sign. And I had been there when he saved her life.

Yes, this happened in North Carolina. We were driving to Miami to visit my aunt Lily. My father wanted to make time, but it was so hot. *Please, please,* I begged, let's stop at a beach. We all went into the ocean. Now, my mother was no swimmer. At home she paddled about in the lake pretending to do the breaststroke, but if you dove under and looked, you could see that her feet were planted firmly on the bottom. My father did the breaststroke, too, but he knew how to swim. He could also float on his back and stick his feet up out of the water; I'd grab on to his toes and he'd tow me along.

So we'd been in the ocean for a while—me, my cousin Bobby, my father and mother—and when we came out to sit on the beach there were only three of us. Where was Mama? I looked around. She was out there, beyond the breakers, waving her arms in the most comical way. I have to admit it, I started to laugh. I couldn't stop laughing. My father hadn't seen her yet, and he didn't know *what* I was laughing at; I was laughing so hard I couldn't speak. I'm *sure* it was hysteria. I pointed. He dove into the breakers and pulled her in. She would have drowned, I know it, and at what point, I always wonder, would I have stopped laughing?

So what I decided was that even though there were no obvious signs of it—no kisses, no banter, no complicit looks between them; and, from his side, cold silences that sometimes lasted for weeks—that was just their way. There were things I was too young to understand.

Men and women, love and marriage: What a mystery at the center of life! It was invisible to my eye, but apparently, there was no power on earth to equal it. I knew that from soap operas on the radio and from movies. But even people I knew had been at its mercy. From what I heard, my mother's best friend, Rose, had been a happily married woman with a child when Albert appeared.

Albert was on the run. Nothing more romantic than a man on the run, particularly a man who looked like Albert, so handsome in the ascetic mode, all bones and severity, with a bushy crown of black hair, a strong, wiry body. Albert was a physical culturist, a follower of Bernarr MacFadden. He believed in exposing his naked body to cold, eating only nuts and grains, taking exercise every morning. And if this wasn't enough, he was a hero, hunted for his beliefs. With the Bureau of Investigation on his tail, Albert lit out from Philadelphia. Deportation or jail was in the offing, for he was, after all, a Communist. Arriving in Brooklyn, he hid out in the back room of my parents' delicatessen. And then Rose dropped by.

———

Rose is from Brailov, like my mother. She is a little older, and my mother, who tends to be worshipful, worships Rose. Rose is cultured and beautiful. Her hair, when she lets it loose, flows wild and black. Many men have been in love with her, and even after she was married, my own uncle-to-be, Noach (who will marry my aunt Frieda), was mad for her. As far as is known, Rose never gave him a tumble, or encouraged any other admirer, until Albert showed up.

"If you see Albert again, you'll never see your daughter," Rose's distraught husband threatens.

The threat didn't work, because here are Rose and Albert, whom I have known all my life, an old married couple living in the Bronx. To see them now, who would guess at the hot passion that had swept them away?

Would I ever manage to get in on this business? On buses and subways, I looked for the girls who wore engagement rings and wedding rings. They were only nine, ten years older than I was, but *they* were in on it. I stared at their work-weary, subway-riding faces for signs of the secret knowledge. They looked so . . . *ordinary*, and yet their initiation was publicly proclaimed by their rings, and sometimes by their big bellies. Weren't they embarrassed to have everyone *know* that they knew?

My father had given my mother no rings. That was their way. But they *knew*.

"Mama," I'd say. "Tell me how you and Daddy met. Tell me how you knew he was the one." She told me bits and pieces, here and there, until I had a story to tell myself.

———

This is how it begins. A small town called Brailov in a strange place called Ukraine. Some streets are cobblestone, others just dirt. When the rains come in the fall, everything turns to mud. There is a river nearby. In the distance are hills to which fields spread away. In summer the fields are carpeted with wildflowers. In winter the snow is waist-high and then, for many months, the inhabitants of the town huddle in their stone houses warmed by huge tiled stoves.

In this town, many years ago, my mother lived, and also a lovely young girl named Manya. Manya was tall and slender. She wore her thick brown hair in braids, which she wound in a coronet around her head. I can see her walking down the street, wearing an embroidered blouse and a fringed shawl wrapped around her shoulders; gold earrings sparkle as she walks. Manya is gay and charming and quick-witted. Everyone loves her, including the schoolteacher, who is a married man.

One cold, rainy morning in the late autumn of, say, 1912, Manya's parents awake to find their daughter's bed empty. In panic, they search all over town. It's a small town, but not that small.

Meanwhile, in another part of town, the schoolteacher's wife, who has waited all night for her husband to come home, opens her door to a knock. A neighbor hands her a note: *I have gone to America with Manya.* Running through the muddy streets, the poor wife wails her abandonment for all to hear. The town is scandalized for months.

Two years pass. My mother is now sixteen, and it is her turn to go to America, where her older sister, Lily, and brother, Oscar, are waiting for her. In Brooklyn the sisters find a room together. They work in sewing factories, sweatshops. Mama (still only Bella) is desperately homesick. She is haunted by the image of her own mother standing at the door of their house, arms outstretched, calling to her: *Mein kind, where are you going, my child?*

For many months Bella cries herself to sleep each night, grieving for her mother and the family she has left behind, for her language, her friends, her lost courage. She, who had been so lively and bold at home, is now fearful of everything. When she realizes that the other girls in the factory are making four dollars a week while she makes only $3.50, her sense of justice is outraged; she summons her courage. One day she waits until everyone has left the sewing loft for the night. She crosses the empty space, passing silent rows of sewing machines, hearing the echo of her footsteps. At last she stands before her boss's desk. He looks up from his ledger.

"What do you want?"

"Oh. I just wanted to say good night, Mr. Kominsky."

A year, two years go by, and Bella becomes reconciled to her new circumstances. She goes to Brighton Beach on her days off. Other girls from Brailov have emigrated: Rose, Tillie, Minnie. They study English at night school and go to free lectures. And Bella has the protection of Lily, who has always looked out for her. Gingerly, she enters into a new life.

One day, during the slow season in the garment industry, when both sisters had been laid off, Lily decides to go to Philadelphia to visit friends from home. She comes back to Brooklyn full of excitement.

"Guess who I saw in Philadelphia?" she says. "Manya!"

Not only had Lily seen Manya and the schoolteacher, but through them she had met an interesting fellow.

"Manya asked about you," she says to her sister. "Go see her. And you'll meet Isidore. See what you think about him." Lily couldn't stop talking about Isidore.

Bella is eager to see Manya again. She has often thought about her. Such romance! To give up everything for love, to be swept away by passion, never mind the scandal. Would she herself be equal to such a test? (What a romantic girl my mother is! Many years in the future, she will follow every detail of Ingrid Bergman's love affair with Rossellini.)

"I'll go to see Manya," she tells Lily, "but, please, I don't want to meet any strangers."

Once in Philadelphia, Bella is dismayed by the sour underside of romance. Manya has a baby, the schoolteacher is unfaithful, the house reeks of diapers and bitterness.

But soon young Isidore presents himself. He is not tall, but he is sturdy, with wavy, dark hair, a forceful nose, and gray eyes. In truth, his chin is a little weak, but only in profile. He is full of self-confidence; and a joker, a prankster, a real flirt. He has already flirted with redheaded Lily. Maybe she took him too seriously, because now he is flirting with the younger sister. Oh, *she* is a pretty girl, no doubt about it. Small and beautifully made. Big, sleepy hazel-green eyes, long black hair, a full mouth. Shy, but more than ready to laugh at his jokes.

Isidore takes Bella to the train station. "I'll write to you," he says. "I'll come to see you."

"Oh," says Bella, stricken with guilt. "Lily will be so happy to see you."

"I'm coming to see *you*," says Isidore. "Come closer. I have a secret to tell you."

Bella inclines her head. "You're a pretty girl," Isidore whispers. One day he'll say that to me. *Putty gull*, is what I hear.

A few weeks later Isidore is waiting outside Bella's factory. She's working in a glove factory now. He has bought her a present. A small wooden gilt-painted box; on the top, in ornate black lettering, are her initials, *BR*. There is a keyhole, and a key to open it. It is filled with chocolates. There is an augury here: Bella's initials will be the same when they marry; and she has a greedy love of sweets. She accepts the gift and enters Manya's country.

"I won't say anything to Lily," she says. "It will hurt her."

For two or three months they write secretly. Isidore writes to her in care of Tillie. He comes to Brooklyn again and stays with a friend. He and Bella take walks, ride the ferry. Bella lies to Lily.

While they are walking together on a cold winter day, Isidore takes Bella's hand and puts it in his pocket. They walk this way in silence for blocks. Later he writes to her: "Are you serious about me?"

"Would I have let you take my hand in that way if I weren't?" Bella answers. (She is not quite *that* innocent; a boy at home has written poems to her eyes; another fell in love with her on the boat to America.)

They begin to plan for the future. It is 1918. The country is at war. Isidore will enlist in the army; when he is discharged he will be eligible for citizenship. And then, when they marry, Bella will be a citizen, which will enable her to bring the rest of her family to America: two sisters, two brothers, a mother and father have fled Ukraine and are refugees in Bucharest.

It is time to tell Lily.

"So why do you think I would care?" Lily says. "He meant nothing to me." She is cold to her sister for a while, but it passes.

Isidore goes to France: Private Rosenbloom. His discharge papers show that he was at the scene of many battles: Avecourt, Pannes, the Meuse-Argonne, Ypres-Lys. He was not wounded, but he was very hungry, very cold, and all around him men were screaming in pain and dying. When he hears the news of the armistice, he deserts, wishing desperately to avoid the irony of being killed when the war is over.

"So, Rosenbloom," his captain says when he shows up at headquarters days behind the rest of his troop. "You're a dirty Jewish coward." He is threatened with court-martial, but it comes to nothing.

Through these long months, Bella has waited for the mail. A photograph of Isidore arrives, taken somewhere in France. He is very thin and wears a heavy backpack with a rifle slung from it. The inscription on the back reads *Your friend, Isidore.* Bella takes the picture to a photographer's studio and has a photograph of herself taken with Isidore inserted, floating in a dream circle above her head. "Thinking of you," she writes on the back.

A year after his enlistment, Isidore returns to Fort Dix. He has lost thirty pounds. People who knew him before he went to war say that he is a changed man. What has happened to him? Was he gassed? Have the scenes of war embittered him beyond repair? He never talks about it. "What difference does it make?" he says when Bella asks him a question. He is irritable, impatient, angry.

"Don't marry him," says Lily to Bella.

Lily is still jealous, Bella thinks. And, woman-like, she believes she can restore him. Her hand is still in his pocket. It is 1920 when they marry. He is twenty-five, she is twenty-two.

———

It had been more than a week since I'd seen my mother. I kept meaning to go up to the nursing home. It was a pain in the neck, really. The place was all the way up in the Bronx, and by the time I got there and back, a whole day was gone. In the beginning I'd go three times a week, then twice. Each time my mother saw me, she smiled with such joy. "How did you find me, darling?"

Rose was in the same nursing home. Albert had died. When the weather was nice, I took them both out to the patio. They sat side by side in their wheelchairs, not speaking, holding hands.

But now it was December and wouldn't you know it! On the very day I planned to go to the Bronx, there was a huge snowstorm, a northeaster that shut the city down. I had to wait another two days until transportation was back on schedule.

I took a subway that becomes an elevated as it reaches the Bronx. The snow was still white on the ground and on the roofs of the buildings. The dingy Bronx was incandescent. I got off near the end of the line and walked up the long hill to the nursing home. I was thinking about my mother's greeting: her smile, joyful, without reproach, despite my long absence; her invariable question: "But, darling, how did you find me?" My answer: "I'll always find you, Mama."

At the reception desk, I signed the register. The receptionist glanced up. Did a double take.

"Who are you here to see?"

"My mother." What was this? He knew who I was!

"Didn't anyone call you?"

"No. What about?"

My heart was beating. I knew. I *knew.* "What?" I cried. "Tell me, tell me. What! Tell me!"

They took me into a small room. The doctor came. There weren't many details. The night before, she'd vomited after dinner, but at seven in the morning she'd been awake, seemed all right. At eight, when they brought her breakfast, she was dead.

"You're not alone, Mama," I'd told her. "You have me."

"Oh yes," she had said. "That's everything."

They let me see her. She was in her room. It was very cold. The window had been opened wide to stanch the smell of death. Her mouth was open. Someone had closed her eyes. They had wrapped her in a large green plastic bag. They had attached a tag to her toe. They shouldn't have done that.

—

Why was I so afraid they would abandon me? They were always there. Never even a baby-sitter. Yet on winter nights in our city apartment, I was unable to fall asleep until I cracked open my bedroom door. Was the light burning in the kitchen? Was the radio playing? Yes. They hadn't gone. On summer nights my fears evaporated as they sat on the porch, all of them, just outside my room. I lay in bed listening to the murmur of voices, my mother's soft laugh, her "*Shhh, the kid is sleeping,*" my aunt Lily's sharp remarks, the men's monosyllabic conversation, the occasional flare of a match, the creaking of the porch swing. A little way off, on the road, I could see the beams from our neighbors' flashlights moving erratically, like extraterrestrial lights. The stars. The smell of summer. My family, my mother, my father. The mystery at the center of life that held them for seventy-two years.

—

We went outside, my cousins and I, and buried the cremains a few yards from the porch.

NO

—

"Why do you always say no, darling?" my mother used to say. "Someday you'll thank me: Practice the piano . . . don't leave anything on your plate . . . work for half an hour on your handwriting . . . you need a tutor for math . . . make the revolution . . ."

—

Here we are, Mama and I, on the lawn outside our bungalow at the end of a hot, still afternoon in the second summer of war, face-to-face on the green double glider. (I buried her ashes just about where the glider stood.) Mama is sitting, and I am standing between her knees. Over her shoulder, through the mesh of the screen door into the kitchen, I see my plump aunt Frieda standing at the stove. (In her middle age she will be killed by a runaway car.) To my left, on the porch, my bossy aunt Lily, always a bit sickly, is napping on the swing. (She will live to her dotage and beyond.)

At this moment Mama and I, so often at odds, are in thrilling mutuality. She is painting my face. With her lipstick (Tangee Flame), she makes my mouth feel as heavy as honey. She makes red circles on my cheeks, dusts my nose with powder, ties a flower-printed kerchief over my braids, and holds up the mirror. *Behold!* From memory, she has drawn a Russian peasant maiden. In an hour or two my mother and aunts will watch proudly from the audience, and I, on the stage of the day camp, will swing a wooden scythe and sing "Meadowlands" to celebrate the glory of the Soviet people as they turn the Fascist tide.

And here we all are again, a couple of years later, August, the last summer of war. I am in the bathroom, thrilled at the sight of my first menstrual blood; only ten years old, but I know what's happening. I run to the kitchen to tell Mama.

She claps her hands. *Mazel tov!* she cries, and turns to tell my aunts, and my uncles too. Everyone congratulates me. Soon a neighbor comes to our door. *Mazel tov!* he calls. *How does he know?* But his congratulations are for the day's headlines: Russia has entered the war against Japan. History, on two fronts!

When I ask my mother a question about Russia, she says quite severely: "So why do you call it Russia, darling? It's the Soviet Union." Yes, yes I knew that, but I get confused. If I asked, "Where were you born, Mama?" she'd say, "You know where I was born, darling. In Russia." Russian was the language in which she and her sisters told their secrets; Russia—or at least a shtetl in Ukraine—was my heritage. The difference seemed to be that while the Russia of my mother's youth was hell on earth, the Soviet Union is the hope of the world.

The ramifications of this Russian/Soviet business radiated through my life. My very name, the "D" of it, honored Georgi Dimitrov, Bulgarian Communist, Comintern leader, hero of the Reichstag trial, the man who brought us the news of the Popular Front. My heart soared to the Red Army Chorus. I knew all the words to "Ballad for Americans," "Meadowlands," "The Banks Are Made of Marble," "The Four Insurgent Generals" before I knew my ABC's. I was in love with Sonny Speisman, who delivered the *Daily Worker* to our house every summer morning; then I was in love with Ernie Lieberman, who played the guitar. Handsome Ernie with the tight brown curls—with his head thrown back, he aimed his sweet tenor at the ceiling: *There once was a Union Maid / Who never was afraid / Of goons and ginks and company finks / And deputy sheriffs who made the raid.* Who was it who said: Beware the movement that makes its own music? Even today the opening notes from any one of those songs will sweep me away. (As for Ernie, decades later I recognized him on the checkout line at Zabar's; to general amusement, I call out, "Ernie! I loved you more than life itself!" He mouths, "Who are *you?*")

Anyway, this is what I take in with my mother's milk, but I am an ignorant, uninstructed child. "Trotskyite" is a well-known curse, but what does it mean? I don't even know that there was such a *person* as Trotsky. It is all as arcane as sex.

Actually, information about sex is easier to come by. From Nina, for example, one of three sisters, who comes running to me and her youngest sister, Irene. "I found prophylactics in the drawer on Daddy's side of the bed."

Irene and I look blank.

"Stupid! The man uses them when they don't want to have a baby." Nina is filled with disgust. "You'd think *three times* would have been *enough* for them!"

Without the picture on the jigsaw-puzzle box, how do you know what the pieces mean? When I think I have an inkling, I test my mother.

"Mama, what's rape?"

"Oh," she says. "It's when a boy kisses a girl and she doesn't want him to."

Is that *all*?

I listen when adults talk. I pick up words and phrases and sentences. I hear "Bolshevik," and "Stalin," and "the Party," and "class struggle," pronounced with reverence. I hear "Trotskyite," and "objectively an agent of Fascism," and "reactionary," and "class enemies" pronounced hatefully. Sometimes people who appeared in earlier conversations as "comrades" become "right-wing deviationists." My mother's cousin Sylvia explains why she will not be going to medical school after all: "They think I can do better work organizing."

Who are *they*?

"What are we, Mama?"

"We're Jewish, darling."

"No, I mean are we Democrats or Republicans?"

"You could say we're progressives."

Is that *it*?

I *love* this place where we spend our summers, and my winter school vacations too. We have an outhouse, no running water, a woodstove. My father, who can do anything, built this house. My real life happens here, sixty miles upstate, at this colony for "Workers and Professionals Only," as it advertises itself, meaning: Nobody is allowed who employs—read "exploits"—labor. (There was a small businessman who misrepresented himself as a worker. He was expelled when it was discovered that he had three employees who were on strike.)

But from September through June, when, during the 1940s, we lived at the upper edge of Harlem, my real identity goes into hiding. We still read the *Daily Worker,* but now I have to walk blocks to buy it at a distant newsstand and spend an extra nickel for the *New York Post* to wrap it in for the dangerous walk back home. When Miss Ferguson, my dreadful sixth-grade teacher, tells us to bring in the newspapers our parents read, I hesitate only between the *Post* and *P.M.* and settle on the *Post* as the safer bet.

My classmates are Irish, Italian, Negro: *Americaaaaaan,* as Paul Robeson sang in celebration of premature multiculturalism. On my block—167th Street, between Amsterdam and Edgecombe Avenues—everyone is Italian until suddenly, after a summer away, we return to find that all the Italians have gone and everyone is Negro. At my school—a Gothic fortress on Broadway and 168th Street—almost everyone is some variety of Catholic—or Negro.

Now, I know the story of the Scottsboro Boys. I know that among the oppressed and exploited proletariat (with whom we are as one) the Negro people rank highest and are to be most esteemed. I have heard the talk about Jim Crow and The Negro Question and The Necessity to Root Out White Chauvinism. I have sung the songs of Leadbelly. But here's my problem: Negro children just don't like me. When I was three or four years old and we lived on Stebbins Avenue in the Bronx, my little playmate Shirley announced one day: "My mama says I can't play with you no more because you're white trash."

"Mama, Shirley says I'm white trash."

"That's just an expression, darling."

In fourth grade, May and Edna have the desks on either side of me. On a test day, May goes to the bathroom. An evil breeze blows her test paper to the floor. She comes back, sees her paper, and stares hard at me.

"What?" I whisper.

"You threw my paper on the floor!" she hisses.

"I didn't!"

"You did so. Fuck your mother."

What does this mean? Is it just an expression?

"Same to you," I say.

May and her four friends (her gang; I have no gang) circle me after school.

"She said 'fuck your mother,' " May explains.

I start to run. Edna sticks out her foot. I trip. My hands and knees are scraped raw. Someone shoves me, someone else hits me. I run and run until I run flat into a lady, who puts herself between me and my pursuers and takes me home.

And I tell no one.

"Oh! What *happened* to you?" Mama says.

"I fell, Mama."

"Be more careful, darling."

I just have this feeling that Mama won't take my side, that ideology—though I am years from knowing this word—will interfere with simple justice. I believe that, somehow, Mama will make it my fault. Suppose I had told her the story: the test paper blown to the floor, the words exchanged, etc. I swear she would have said something like: "Darling, you must work to eradicate white chauvinism in yourself; as the vanguard of the working class, we must show the Negro masses how to take their place among the international proletariat."

If you think I'm laying it on too thick, listen to this: I spent my thirteenth and fourteenth summers at Camp Wochica (Workers' Childrens' Camp, in case you thought it was your standard inauthentic Indian name). Our camp song was sung to the tune of "Oh Moscow Mine," and our project was to dig a new cesspool for the camp. (Talk about the theory of surplus value!) I learned to smoke cigarettes during those summers, to wield a shovel, and gratefully, with Karl and Anatole, I learned more about sex. For the same money I had instruction in detecting hidden manifestations of white chauvinism.

Once a week, more often if circumstances demanded, we were subjected to sessions of self-criticism so that we might admit to errors in our behavior, and have the opportunity to point out errors in the behavior of our fellow campers. These sessions were led by our counselor, Elsie, in a sort of mini-trial format designed to, as the not very catchy slogan went, "root out every manifestation of open or concealed white chauvinism in our ranks."

Elsie to an unwary camper: "Sasha! Did you offer Joan [Negro] a slice of watermelon?"

Sasha: "Well, yes, but we had watermelon for dessert that day . . ."

Elsie: "But Bernie reported that you passed Joan an *extra* slice. Do you admit this?"

Sasha: "She asked me . . ."

Elsie: "So! You blame Joan for her own oppression!"

Poor Joan burst into tears, maybe from embarrassment,

or maybe realizing at last the extent of her own oppression. I passed her a tissue.

Elsie: "And you! What right do you have to act as Joan's friend when you have *never* made a special effort to gain her friendship?"

You know what would have happened if I had made such an effort? *A transparent attempt to avoid charges of chauvinism!*

Time passed and I graduated into the Labor Youth League, successor to the Young Communist League. We met in a firetrap tenement on the Lower East Side. At one meeting I got into an argument with our leader, whom we called Rooster (long neck, bobbing Adam's apple). I can't remember what the argument was about: probably something about the wording of one of those jargon-filled leaflets we handed out on street corners to the working class, who (misled by False Consciousness) despised us. I sat in my chair in that cold, badly lit, dirty room, brooding on my grievances. I hated handing out those leaflets to passersby, who at best ignored my out-thrust arm and at worst snarled or even spat at me. I hated being monitored for deviations in thinking and, in turn, being a heresy hunter myself. I was at that moment in a dark, smoky room, and my life was feeling just as airless. I still didn't understand what Trotsky had done that was so horrible, for God's sake! I got up to leave the meeting.

"Sit down!" Rooster called. "A Negro comrade is speaking!"

I was sixteen. It was 1951. The Hollywood writers had been blacklisted; people had informed or refused to inform in front of HUAC; Alger Hiss had been convicted of perjury; the Rosenbergs had been arrested; my English teacher at Seward Park High School had been fired for subversive activities; family friends were being followed by the FBI, whose agents sometimes knocked on our door to try to ask my mother questions. For lack of anyone else to ask, I sometimes asked her questions myself.

"Mama, why did Stalin have Trotsky assassinated?"

"Who says he was assassinated, darling? Some deranged person killed him."

"Mama, why did Stalin sign the pact with Hitler?"

"That was a tactic, darling. To give the Soviet Union more time to prepare for the war."

"Mama, are the Rosenbergs Communists?"

"They're progressives, darling. They're being persecuted because they believe in justice for all people, and because they're Jews."

"Is Alger Hiss a Communist?"

"Of course not. He's a liberal person who's opposed to the warmongers."

"What about Whittaker Chambers? He says *he* was a Communist."

"He's a very sick man."

In this time of trouble, was I a rat leaving a sinking ship? Who was I, if not who I always had been? Who would my friends be? What would we talk about? How would I learn a new vocabulary? And *what* would replace the central mission of my life, to man the barricades when the revolution came?

———

A few months after my mother died, I dreamed we were together in a foreign country, hurrying along a path toward her childhood home. When we reached the house where she had been born, we found it deserted and derelict: wooden plank walls were splayed apart; the roof gaped; a few half-starved animals wandered around an overgrown yard. In dismay we started back toward the town, hoping to find someone who could tell us what had happened to the inhabitants of the house. The light began to fade. I saw that my mother had crossed the road. She was walking very quickly now, each step leaving me farther behind. I called to her to wait; I was in terror of being left alone in this strange country, where only she knew the language. Then it was pitch-dark. I could not see my mother anymore. I shouted, "Mama! Mama!" but she was gone.

Of course I was dreaming about my mother's death. I

was still grief-stricken and bereft. But when the sound of my own voice woke me, I knew in what country she had abandoned me.

And then I remembered that I had first abandoned her.

It was 1948, the year Henry Wallace ran for president. Mama and I were at Madison Square Garden. We were at the very top of the house, looking down on the brightly lit arena. Standing at the center of the stage was Vito Marcantonio, *our* congressman. Oh, he was a *wonderful* speaker, my mother always said, a fiery orator. That man knew how to work a crowd. And as he spoke, his feet stamping, his arms waving, his voice growing louder and more rhythmic as he approached the climax of his speech, the entire audience rose to its feet, chanting with him, roaring approval. And I was on my feet too, transported, at one with the crowd, melted into it, my voice its voice. I was lost.

And suddenly, without willing it, as the crowd still roared, I came to myself. I felt very cold. I looked at Mama, still on her feet, clapping, chanting. *Who was she* now? About Marcantonio, I thought: *He could tell us to do anything now, and we'd do it.* I was out of there. I was history.

No, I said. But not so Mama could hear.

COUSIN MEYER'S

AUTOBIOGRAPHY

—

When *my cousin Meyer (twice removed)*
reached the age of eighty-seven, he com-
mitted suicide. His health was bad, his
prospects grim, and everyone said he was a
man who looked facts in the face. "You
will need a car to attend to everything, so
better drive here," he wrote to his daughter.
"My door will be unlocked, get somebody

to walk in with you. . . ." He gave instructions about his cremation, and about important papers "in the white tin box." Among these papers was a manuscript addressed "To Whom It May Concern."

—

I am a simple man. I am uneducated. Yet I lived long and kept my eyes open. In my youth I read books: Chernyshevsky, Bakunin, Lasalle. I formed opinions. From my readings and my experience of the world, I came to the conclusion that only the system of socialism could liberate mankind, because it would abolish the system of exploitation of man by man. Could it be that I was wrong? Of this I will never be convinced! After all, didn't I endure hardship? Didn't I struggle for my living while others profited from my misery? Yes, I had convictions. I stuck by my convictions.

Now. To begin at the beginning. I was born on March 4, 1893, in a cold, dark room in a small town called Brailov in the Ukraine. I never knew my father. He dropped dead when I was in the womb. My mother already had six children, and there was no milk in her breasts for me. How I cried with hunger when she held me to suckle those empty breasts! That I survived at all was a miracle. When I was eleven years old, my mother took me to the city of Zsmerkinka and left me there to work in a store of flour and grains, just for the price of my room and board. How cruel they were to me! I was still a child. I longed for my home and family. I cried from hunger and cold.

Poverty and hunger formed me. And history too. When I was a young boy in 1905, a revolution failed. There were many pogroms in our area. Once, when the Cossacks came, my mother put my sister in the stove. Still, we had some laughs. Every other Sunday we had a fair in Brailov. People made jokes: About Reb Mates, who was cross-eyed, we used to say that he looks on onions but buys potatoes. And I remember one Saturday night in summer when a group of us boys hired a boat and went rowing on the lake. We sang such songs! *Carry away my soul into the blue far distance.* It seems like only yesterday, the beautiful dreams of our promising youth. Who, *who* is still alive to remember that Saturday night!

One question I have always asked myself: Why do we not all agree and put our efforts to learn how to distribute the great wealth of our planet equally to all mankind? This world of ours would then become a paradise on earth!

Well, to go on. There was no future for a poor boy in Brailov, so I went to Odessa. My mother warned me of the bad women who walked the streets there: "I am your mother," she said. "It is my duty to warn you that you could get infected with a terrible disease. Your nose will fall down in small pieces. You might get blind. In the end it will reach your brain. You get insane and soon you die in terrible agonies." Believe me, I listened to my mother and never forgot her warning my whole time in Odessa.

When I was twenty years old, I went to America. This was just before the Great War broke out. I sailed on a dirty, miserable ship. Eighteen days later we saw land. It was like Moses seeing the land of Israel, except for the skyscrapers. Then my struggles really began: one job after another for a few pennies a week. I lived for a while with my cousin Mendel under the elevated in the Bronx. I got used to it. First I worked in a steam laundry, then I got a pushcart and sold remnants. What didn't I do in the land where gold was supposed to lie on the streets? The exploitation at that time in America was inhuman. There were no unions to protect workers.

And then we heard the great news! Czar Nicholas lost his throne and his head! Lenin and Trotsky made a victorious revolution! No more Capitalism! No more private property! We danced in the streets. But we knew their road would not be an easy one.

As if to celebrate this glorious event, my son was soon born. I was then working as a streetcar conductor, then I drove a milk wagon seven days a week. Always my wages stayed just a few pennies ahead of starvation. A few years later I had a daughter. I loved my son, but every father loves also to have a little girl. Such a beautiful little girl. Cheeks like two red roses, and big shining eyes.

It occurs to me that I forgot to put in that I got married. If I didn't mention this before, it's because the less said about it the better. My wife and I didn't get along. Whose fault was that? It was one of those things. A man isn't always lucky in his marriage. I loved a woman, but she was not my wife; I'll come to that. However, I did my best for my family. I had a chicken farm, and believe me I sweated blood there. My chickens froze to death one night and I was wiped out clean. Then I bought a grocery store that burned to the ground. I picked myself up and went on. What else could I do?

My children were growing up and I was proud of them. My boy and my girl were smart children. When the time came, I was able to put them through college. Even in the Depression, when people were on breadlines, I managed so we never went hungry. What happened to this greatest, richest land in the world? What happened to "a chicken in every pot"?

When my boy was fifteen, I decided to take a trip to my

old home to see my mother before she died. I also wanted to see the new system, the Soviet system. To tell you the truth, I also had a furtive hope to remain there and thus liberate myself from my very unhappy marriage.

Well, when I say that I went to the Ukraine in 1932, I don't have to tell you what I found. Stalin's collectivization. When I arrived in Brailov, the entire Jewish population was on the verge of total starvation. The Depression in America was nothing compared to it. My mother was emaciated, lifeless. I hardly recognized her. She was so weak she could not raise herself to greet me. *What happened to my mother?* Where has her hearty humor gone? She did not even have tears left in her eyes, they had dried out. And my sisters! My brothers! I had heard some rumors, but this I could not believe. I unpacked my suitcase, which I had filled with as much food as I could carry.

Where are the pots? I asked my mother. "Pots?" she said. "We have no pots. We sold the pots. What do we need pots for? We have nothing to cook."

That night in my old home I could not fall asleep. It looked to me like a nightmare. Outside my window I heard cats and dogs crying with hunger. The next morning I walked out to see once more my childhood place. What did I see? Abandoned horses, tiny like dogs, starving, all their ribs showing, standing motionless on the streets, full of sores, their eyes and their sores all covered with flies. The few people with enough strength to leave their houses walked slowly, aimlessly.

I asked myself the question: Must this be the terrible price that people had to pay to bring about a better society? I could not stay with my family more than three days. It would kill me. I had to leave them to their own fate. In my heart I said: Good-bye, my dear family; good-bye, my Russian friends. I wish you from the bottom of my heart great success in your hard task.

You see, we must always remember that the Soviet leaders were the first in the history of mankind who took upon themselves the great task of building a new society on communist principles. We will admit they made lots of mistakes. They were moving along unexplored paths. Even the Bible tells us that before God created this world of ours, there was darkness and disorder. I kept my faith. When people asked me, What about the sufferings and sacrifices of so many human beings? I have always been able to reply with confidence: After all, since the beginning of history, millions of people were killed in wars in the interests of kings and imperialist bandits. True, the Russian revolution came about with a terrible price in deaths and in sufferings—hunger and starvation. But it was all in the interests of the *people*. To end the dog-eat-dog system. It is too bad that this generation had to pay such a terrible price, but it was unavoidable. They did not die in vain; they fought to bring for their children a better life. Isn't this so? This I will believe until my dying day.

And even this terrible suffering grew pale next to the sufferings of the war. Of course I heard nothing from my family during the war. When it was all over, I wrote to my niece Lyuba to find out what had happened to my family. This is what she wrote to me:

> I am worried that my letter will make you sick, dear uncle, but I can't bear it alone. Our town was occupied by the Germans in July 1942. There were four slaughterings in our town. The first was on the 12th of February, 1942. No more Papa, no more Mama, no brothers and sisters, no one. All three thousand Jews in Brailov were killed by the Nazi murderers. They declared my home *Judenrein*.

These things are beyond imagining. For many years I have had nightmares about the sufferings of my family. If only, if only I could have saved them, if I could have known. . . . If it counts against me in the reckoning of my life that I did not try to save them while it was still possible, so be it.

To change the subject for the better, there is another thing I must tell. On this trip I took to the Soviet Union in 1932, I met a girl on the boat. I was then thirty-nine years old, but I looked younger. She was twenty-nine, a social worker from Canada. A nice girl. I was the first man in her love life. I told her that I was a married man with two lovely children, but she did not care. She wanted to experience life, to enjoy herself. For two months we lived together as husband and wife. When we came back to New York, I told her the honeymoon is over. I would not abandon my two lovely children.

Of course it will occur to readers of this, my autobiography, that I was ready to abandon my children and stay forever in the Soviet Union when I thought everything would be rosy there. Yes. I admit that. But in that case I would have been helping to build the socialist dream, so I felt I could make such a sacrifice. Better to be honest here: If I stayed there, I would not have had to face my wife and children. But when I saw the misery in Brailov, I realized I had lived in America too long. I was spoiled. I had not the stamina to withstand the hardships of Soviet life. As for the girl, Ethel, maybe I didn't want to start with another woman, another family, more responsibilities. Yes, I was selfish and spoiled.

When we parted, Ethel cried. But she believed me when I said my duty comes first to my family. I didn't forget her for a long time.

Thirty-six years passed by. Life passed by. My hair turned white. My children brought forth a third generation, five lovely, decent grandchildren they gave me. Before I looked around I was an old man. Life had nothing more in store for me, right? Wrong.

One night I was sitting watching the news. The announcer was telling about Vietnam. I saw that the ground was covered with old people, women, and children, some dead, some on their knees begging for mercy from our boys. I broke down and cried. God, I cried, is there no justice in this world of ours? Why do we kill and murder poor people who have never done us any wrong? Just then the phone rang. Right away I recognized her voice. "Ethel! Where are you?" I said. She was visiting friends in my city.

My wife was alive, but we lived separate by then. Ethel came to my apartment. She was gray, but still an attractive woman. She had had an interesting life. She lived in Israel on a kibbutz and was married there, but divorced her husband because he had other women. After the war she went to Germany to help settle the concentration camp survivors. She married later, again, in Canada. When she came to see me her husband was still alive, but he was a sick man.

Ethel spent ten days with me. She would not allow me to touch her. She did not want to deceive her husband. "I respect him," she said, "even though I don't love him as I loved you. I wanted to see you once more, but my duty is to my sick husband."

She went back home to Canada, but life brought us together once more. When her husband died she came to live with me. Age was not an obstacle to our love. It took another form than in our younger days. It was something I have no word for. We walked, we talked, we could still touch each other. We agreed on everything. We had only one year together before she, too, died, but it was the happiest year of my entire life.

I have written down everything I can remember. My life began in a cold, dark room in old Russia. I knew great poverty and hunger there. I lived through wars and a great revolution. I was all my life on the side of the underprivileged, on the side of justice for the poor people that are under the heel of the richer classes. As a husband I wasn't ideal, but I tried to be a good father and grandfather. For a little while I had happiness in love. This is my autobiography. In the bottom drawer are copies for whoever wants one.

BEYOND THE PALE

—

You know what a pale is? Probably you do. I had to look it up. A pale is a picket, as in fence. All my life when I heard about the Pale of Settlement I imagined snow falling softly, perpetually, on Jewish villages, once upon a time.

—

We lived in Washington Heights because my father had a garage there. Daddy liked us to live near where he worked so that he could run home when he forgot something; if business was slow, he could take a snooze. When that happened, he'd send my mother to watch the garage. It never occurred to me how strange this was. Driving is what the garage business is all about, and Mama didn't know how to drive. A customer comes, he leaves his car on the ramp to be parked; another customer comes, he waits for someone to retrieve his car from behind three other cars. Mama couldn't even pump gas. She'd sit reading in the office—a makeshift cubicle with a kerosene stove—and by and by a customer would show up. Then another. "Just a minute. Just a minute," Mama would say frantically. "The boss had an emergency. He'll be back soon."

"What's the emergency?" a customer once said to me.

"Oh, no emergency, he's just sleeping," I said.

Mama heard that and pulled me aside. "I'm not going to tell Daddy what you said."

—

When I was about seven years old, we moved to the corner of Edgecombe Avenue and 167th Street, which was a little closer to the garage. By this time we'd lived in four or five different apartments in the city, but this new one is the first I remember whole.

Our building was like the others on the street, a six-story

walk-up. We lived on the third floor. The apartment was more hall than rooms: You opened the front door into a long, long, windowless hallway, so narrow that even my little arms could touch the sides without straightening. At the very end of the hall was the bathroom; to the left of the bathroom, the kitchen, to the right, the living room. My mother and father slept in the living room. My room opened directly from theirs. Looking east, out my window, I could see the Harlem River and the Bronx beyond it, and on game nights, the sky blazed with lights from the Polo Grounds.

We lived on Edgecombe Avenue for about six years. Mornings at seven, while we ate breakfast, and evenings at six, while we had supper, the Second World War played on the kitchen radio.

"Daddy," I said. "What will they talk about on the radio when the war is over?"

"Don't worry about it," he said.

President Roosevelt died on Edgecombe Avenue. When Mama and I came home that afternoon, she went to the bathroom and I went to the kitchen and turned on the radio.

"Mama," I called, after I'd listened a minute. "They're saying that President Roosevelt died."

Through the closed door she called back, "No, darling. They're just talking about what would happen *if* he died."

She came into the kitchen and we listened together and began to cry.

It was funny about President Roosevelt. We loved him, but it seemed to me that I could remember a time when we didn't. Something about him being a "warmonger" and the war being "imperialist." Now, of course, all anybody talked about was Roosevelt and Stalin and Churchill, our Great Allied Leaders. This state of affairs had lasted so long that I was sure my memory was playing tricks. So I said I would give President Roosevelt my cat.

This is how that happened. I loved my cat, Cutie, more than anything, but it's true she was a nuisance, always running up and down the fire escape, crying to be let in or out, staying away all night, coming home with her ears torn. One day my father came home from the garage and I heard him say, in a low voice, to my mother, "Where's the kid?"

I was in my room. He came in, which he didn't often do, and sat down on my bed.

"You know what happened today?" This was going to be important.

"Faye Emerson came to the garage." I knew who Faye Emerson was; everybody did. She was the beautiful actress married to President Roosevelt's son Elliott.

"Faye Emerson said that President Roosevelt heard about Cutie and he wants to take her to live at Hyde Park."

President Roosevelt! Hyde Park! I could hardly believe it! Such honor! My Cutie, living with the Roosevelts on a big estate, playing with Fala! Of course she must go! There was the war effort to consider!

So one day, not long after she requested my cat, Faye Emerson (though probably she sent her chauffeur) came to get Cutie. That's what must have happened, because when I came home from school, Cutie was gone. Don't you think that's what happened?

———

Edgecombe Avenue was a hill, with the Polo Grounds at the bottom and us at the top. It was like a suburb of Harlem where richer Negroes lived. Our building was just an ordinary tenement, but there were apartment houses farther down Edgecombe that were palatial, with marble lobbies and elevators and doormen. Joe Louis lived on Edgecombe, but I never saw him.

On our actual block, which ran from Edgecombe to Amsterdam Avenue, there were only Italians. Italians sat on the stoops and spoke Italian, they called out the windows in Italian, they drank red wine from water glasses and ate Italian ices. Then, there was that September when we came back from Goldens Bridge to find that all those Italians had morphed into Negroes.

Three long blocks to the west of Edgecombe was Broadway. But before you got there, you had to cross Amsterdam Avenue, where the trolleys ran, and then St. Nicholas Avenue. Those streets, and the cross streets, were Spanish and Irish streets. Jews lived farther uptown on Broadway and along Fort Washington Avenue. Each block on the route to Broadway was a separate state, with borders to be negotiated.

Like the day I was walking west on 169th Street on my way to see my aunt Rachile and my cousin Vivian. They lived on 174th, just off Broadway. Suddenly I found myself surrounded by the Irish. (It's silly to say you can't tell what people are by looking at them; I knew they were Irish and, they, as you'll see in a minute, knew what I was.)

"What are you doing on this block?" the biggest kid said.

"I'm just going to Broadway."

"I bet you're a Jew," he said. And then the chorus, "Yeah, she's a *Jew!*" The circle tightened.

Every nerve in my body screamed *NO I'M NOT!*, but it was as plain as the nose on my face that no matter what I said, the die was cast. I might as well get something out of the beating. I took a deep breath. "Yeah," I said. "And

what are you going to do about it!" As I tell it now, it was
worth it.

———

When I was grown up, I met a guy named Jack (actual
name), who'd gone to DeWitt Clinton High School with
James Baldwin. Jack thought that this connection reflected
well on him. He managed to mention it often, apropos or
not: "Jimmy Baldwin said . . . When Jimmy Baldwin and I
went . . ." And we, his friends, had the distinct feeling that
should you say to Jack something on the order of "Hey, Jack,
did you have any other Negro friends besides James Baldwin?", Jack would answer, "*Negro? I* never noticed he was
Negro!"

Well, Mama was a little like Jack. If someone said to her,
"So you live in a Negro neighborhood?" Mama would say,
"We live in a neighborhood of working people."

Of course she was under orders. In those days no one (and
by "no one" I mean we Communists) knew when he or she
might be accused of White Chauvinism. Somebody would
report you; you were brought up on charges before local
leaders. You searched your memory: *What* did I *do?*

"*Didn't you ask Comrade Jones if he wanted his coffee
black?*"

It was like those Irish kids who beat me up: Once the gang

formed, you might as well agree to the accusation, for all the good denial would do you.

———

So now I was getting older and junior high school loomed. Our address would funnel me directly into Stitt Junior High, two blocks away, on Edgecombe Avenue.

I said, "Mama, I don't want to go."

I was scared. I had *reason*. And, of course, the reason was unspeakable; in fact, neither Mama nor I mentioned the fact that ninety percent of the kids at Stitt were Negro. School was a dangerous place. You needed allies. And I already knew (and maybe Mama even remembered from her own school days among the Christians) that allies were more likely to come in your own color and creed.

Considering her choices—for daughter, against doctrine—Mama was brave. She took a chance that the comrades wouldn't notice, and in my last year of grade school she told school authorities that I was going to live with my aunt on 174th Street. From that address I would be poised for a more congenial junior high—that is, a school that was maybe forty percent Negro, the rest divided between Spanish, Jewish, Italian, Irish. Mike Lugo was Italian.

———

I'd been in love before. With Freddy Bloom, who left me waiting in front of the Coliseum Theatre on 181st Street on a cold spring day and broke my heart. With Richard Borrow, who was in my sixth grade class and liked another girl better. With Barry Axelrod, the park director, who wrote a play and made me his star. (I had such a bad case of stage fright that I peed in my pants onstage, in front of everyone, and was too ashamed to ever speak to him again.)

Mike Lugo was a rough, tough Catholic boy, beyond the Pale beyond any doubt. I was his girl; nobody messed with me when he was around. My association with him brought me a place in the world, and enough friends so that I was going to have a thirteenth birthday party.

———

We were on our way to Macy's to buy a dress for my party when I said to my mother, "Please, Mama. Do it the regular way."

I meant that just this once she shouldn't humiliate me. She and my aunts had a technique for buying clothes for special occasions. First, of course, you chose a dress. But a major consideration in making your choice was whether the tags were in a position to be easily tucked in, because, once worn for the occasion, the dress was to be returned. The transaction was filled with anxiety at every step. Would the tags dangle from the sleeve when worn? Would you get a stain on the dress? When returned, would the salesgirl notice that the dress had been worn?

"But, darling," Mama said. "When will you ever wear it again?"

"*Please*, Mama." So we bought a dress outright, a black taffeta number, princess-style, with a sweetheart neckline. My first black dress.

—

I don't remember very much about the party. I'm sure I was nervous. I have an image of a crowd in our so-called living room. I know that Sheila Minnick and Anna Hernandez and her brother Ray were there, and Diana Contafacilis too. I think my parents had agreed to stay in the kitchen and let us close the doors to the living room. But did we have music? Did we dance? What did we eat and drink?

All I remember (because, really, what is a party about if not about sex?) is that Mike Lugo and I went into my bedroom.

He closes the door. The lights are off and we're lying on my bed, kissing, crushing my black taffeta dress, and I'm thinking how lucky that it doesn't have to go back to Macy's. Mike is breathing urgently. He whispers something I can't quite hear.

What? I whisper back.

Can I touch your breast? he says.

Oh no, I say.

We kiss some more, and then he says, Promise me something.

What?

If you won't let me, promise you won't ever let anybody.

I promise, I say just as the door opens, and I see Mama framed in the light.

"Shame!" she cries.

———

Not long after that we moved from Edgecombe Avenue to Grand Street, on the Lower East Side. I think Mama was glad to get me out of Washington Heights. But it was a little late. I'd lived too long outside the Pale, associated too intimately with the Other, knew too well the advantages of such association. I knew altogether too much. I knew Cutie had gone to the pound, not Hyde Park. The cat was out of the bag, so to speak.

LILY'S BOND

—

My aunt Lily had not been lucky in love. First she fixed her heart on my father, and we've seen how that turned out. Next she set her sights on handsome Victor; he chose her youngest sister, Rachile. As far as I know she never fell for Norman, who was quite taken with Rachile, who in turn steered him to Frieda.

One way or another, all Lily's sisters were married when the Depression hit. At that time, as it happened, she was earning better than any of her sisters' husbands, and they had to borrow from her. That circumstance gave her some of her old cachet, as when, in the days before all those husbands, she'd pretty much run the family show.

In her work, at least, Lily had lucked into a good thing. She sold lingerie door-to-door. Now ask yourself: What kind of woman could afford, maybe even *need*, expensive silk and lace underwear in hard times? Right—Lily had a regular clientele of hookers. They were always in the market for something new, something more provocative, and they paid cash on the spot. I don't know how Lily got into this line of work, but when she fell in love again, in the early 1930s, she gave her route to my mother (to keep warm) and took off for California with a man named Tom. She hoped this would be *it*. Many years later I came across a photograph of the two of them with their arms around each other; somewhere in a sepia Midwest they leaned against Lily's great old car.

"Tell me!" I said to my mother. I'd never seen Lily looking so young and happy.

"It didn't work out," Mama said. "Lily had to take the train home. That was a good thing. She was a terrible driver."

Naturally Lily was dejected, but she retrieved her client list from my mother and went back to work. Not too much later she met Ben.

I like to think that they met through her work: she, arriving at a customer's apartment with her wares; he, on his way out, having paid a pretty penny to admire the wares on and off the model. One look at the redheaded saleslady and he loses his heart. Not likely. Probably it was a match made by a distant relative.

Lily was interested right away. Time was flying and Ben was plausible: the right age—middle thirties—no previous wives, tallish, with regular features, not at all bad-looking. What's more, unlike my father or my uncles Norman and Victor, those rough diamonds, Ben was a man of some refinement. He wrote poetry and played the violin. Lily was bringing culture to the family, and about time someone did! To earn a living—not much of a living, may it be said (and it was)—Ben gave music lessons.

He was a strange bird to land among these brothers-in-law. *Poetry! music!—he earns a living from this?* The brothers-in-law, often at odds among themselves, were united in suspicion. What is he, a sissy? my uncle Norman wondered. Maybe worse! my father suggested. And another thing: The man seemed to have no politics! Of course he was after Lily for her money; *that* they could understand. Well, just who did he think he was dealing with! Wasn't Lily's money a *family* resource?

Poor Ben. In the old country, he would have had respect. He would have been a scholar, a rabbi even, entitled to a wife who kept him while he spent all day at his books. And it wasn't fair to Lily to speak of her as if she had no attractions apart from her earnings. My father and Victor may have passed up their chance with her, but she was a nice-looking woman, even if no beauty like the other sisters. She knew how to take care of herself. She wore makeup, her wavy auburn hair was stylishly bobbed, and she was always fashionably dressed compared to her sisters, who claimed to despise bourgeois fashion and female artifice. ("As long as it's clean," Mama would say whenever I balked at a hand-me-down; my father's notion of a compliment was "It's neat," meaning exactly that.)

Of course Lily did have some drawbacks. She had inherited a family tendency to bronchitis; as for personality, let's say that she was something of a scold. "You look like a greenhorn, Belle," she nagged at my mother, until Mama cut off the black braids that had adorned her like a coronet and got a horrible perm instead.

The worst thing Lily did for my mother's good was to

burn all her papers. That was during the McCarthy years: Mama's compositions, essays, letters—all up in smoke. Poor Mama. Those papers meant the world to her; they were her real American citizenship papers. She had earned them in hard-won months at Brookwood Labor College, at Bryn Mawr Summer School for Working Women, at Barnard Summer School where, always, she was the favorite of her teachers, praised for her intelligence and her writing. (But that's another story.) She never forgave Lily.

To get back to Ben. His brothers-in-law may have been a little crude in their judgment, but there *was* something creepy about my uncle Ben. Something unpleasant about his pale, slick skin, something Uriah Heepish in his elaborate deference. Now that I think of it, I wonder if his unfortunate snuffle was his way of showing that he was looking down his nose at us: With closed mouth, he would push air through his nose with a sound something like a flooded engine—if you liked him you could assume he was clearing his nasal passages; if not, you could take it as his opinion of you.

In my mother, though, Ben sensed a sympathetic soul. She admired music (in theory only; in real life she was tone-deaf), she valued education, and she revered the printed word. Ben took to writing her long letters.

Dear Bella,

With the winter months to be here soon, you will proba-
bly need reading matter to while away the howling win-
ter nights. Here are a few pages that might help you out.
There are plenty of people reading my scribbling, so you'll
merely join the flock. I hope your response won't be too
unfavorable . . .

You see the problem. Those mixed messages—the desperate plea for understanding, the defensive offensiveness,
the readiness with which he was prepared to take umbrage.
What a sensitive plant he was! Who could assuage him?
When one of Ben's thick envelopes arrived, my mother
sighed deeply: Once again a wrong had been done him. But
she always read the letter, and she always answered. Not to
answer would only add another wrong, which would duly appear in his next letter.

—

For many years Lily and Ben lived in the Highbridge section
of the Bronx. Two little rooms for just the two of them. They
had no children. Lily worked as a saleslady, Ben gave a few
violin lessons. They weren't spenders. Lily kept a lot of her
money in a joint account with my mother. And, as you'll see,
she had a savings bond destined for Frieda. For Ben, he had

a roof over his head and his meals. Sometimes I imagined the sounds that filled the little apartment when they were alone: Ben's flooded-engine snuffle, Lily's bronchial cough.

There came a time, some twenty years into the marriage, when Lily's bronchitis worsened. She coughed up blood. Her doctor urged a change of climate. She went to Florida. After a week, she wrote to Ben: "Very, very good, Ben. This air does something to me. It's hot, but it's soothing. People love it here. I love it." A week later she wrote again: "I think I'll stay longer, Ben. I feel good here." And two weeks later: "I want to stay here. I am not coming back to New York. This is the place where I have to live."

Ben was beside himself. What was the meaning of this? Was Lily leaving him? Did she mean for him to join her? Myself, I think she meant to get rid of him but lost her nerve. Because in answer to his panicked letter, she wrote: "It's up to you, Ben. Think it over and think hard. Answer me."

I remember [he wrote to Mama] *standing, looking around me in our little apartment, the small living room with the little kitchen behind the screen, the few chairs, the couch where Lily and I sat—how long?—many years, living our life here, confronting our problems, planning our days. In the bedroom the bookcase near the bed, all so familiar, and all to be gone, never to be seen again. Limbs one is born with, and other parts one annexes through life, and all become part of one, and one retains some and must sever himself from the others. And a strange organ, the heart, too, immediately involved in all of this. It can flutter with no weight at all, or be loaded down with a ponderous burden. Can gush streams of joy, or discharge a deluge of unhappiness, and can dispense what flavor one desires—bitter or sweet. That day I recall a dribble of fear steal into my body. A premonition? Uncertainty became my companion.*

You can see the man had feeling for the written word, but, oh, the pathos! He was in his fifties by then, with no financial hopes except for the living he eked out with music lessons; with no stomach for life on his own. He faced the truth: He was lost without Lily. She held all the cards—and not only the money. He answered her letter posthaste, forgetting even to assume an attitude. "If Florida is the place for you to live, then it will be my place too. Let me know what to do. How to go about joining you. Because I really don't know how to begin." It was almost a love letter.

So the marriage continued by default. Lily sent detailed instructions about how he was to pack up the apartment. And then she gave him a final task. "Remember the package we keep in Norman's safe," she wrote. "The bond is in it, and also the key to our safety deposit box. Don't get these things until the day before you leave so you will be sure not to lose them. They are everything we have in the world."

Ben had lots of time to contemplate the future as he dismantled the small apartment. The problem was, could he ever reassemble *himself?* He knew no one in Florida, only a cousin and the woman's husband. What was his name? Sam! So shifty-eyed, such a monstrous braggart! He was giving up *everything* by joining Lily, burning all his rickety bridges to life. He burned with resentment too. Well, no point thinking about it, he had no choice.

There wasn't much time left. It was already Wednesday. On Thursday he would have to wait in the apartment for the movers; on Friday morning his train was leaving. It was time to get the package and the key from Norman, retrieve the valuables from the bank, and say good-bye to the family. Suddenly he had tender feelings for the family. He imagined friendly handshakes and good wishes, promises to visit soon. *I'll feel a lot better when I see them, I surely will.*

———

In those days, Norman had a garage. So did my father. In fact, they had once been partners in the garage business. Two pigheaded men in business together? Two pigheaded men, each determined to prevail? Please! Their wives told them that it was a terrible idea, but, being pigheaded, they paid no attention. They split up in less than a year, and then they had to sort out the complications of a partnership gone bad; my father went around bad-mouthing Norman. Naturally, that got back to Frieda, who stormed into our apartment one day and, in front of my mother, let my father have it. He took it sitting down. God, I wish I'd seen that.

Anyway, on the Wednesday before his Friday departure, Ben went off to see Norman. He was uneasy about the errand. Just why, he couldn't have said. He was already at the subway when he rushed back to the apartment to get Lily's letter. That was a clue.

At Norman's garage, Ben feigned nonchalance.

I spoke casually, telling him of our decision to move to Florida, saying I came for the package we had in his safe, since the key to our bank box was there, and also, I said, the bond in which Lily had made Frieda the beneficiary. Lily wanted to have everything, since she didn't know what she may need. I commented on what a job it was making the move and the work it involved.

Busy as I was talking, I didn't notice the peculiar expression on Norman's face. When I did look up, he had his eyes squinting as he peered at me suspiciously, while a frown covered his face. "I don't know. I don't know," he mumbled. Next moment he got up and began pacing back and forth in front of his desk, his eyebrows lowered, his eyes trying to penetrate through me. For a moment it occurred to me that perhaps he didn't have the key to the safe.

"I have it! I have it!" he answered.

I couldn't believe it! He hesitated to give me the package! I hastily took Lily's letter from my pocket and placed it on the desk.

"Here is Lily's letter," I said irritably.

"She didn't write me nothing," he complained. ["Not-*ting"* is actually how Ben rendered the word.] *He stood there obstinately. He didn't even reach for the letter. Did he consider it a forgery?*

He became more conciliatory. He sat down. "You see, Ben," he said. "I'm Lily's guardian. I have to protect her. Come back tomorrow and we'll see."

I looked at him. So. My wife had a guardian! I didn't know that. I wonder what would happen, Bella, if some man told Rosen that he was your guardian? Rosen would probably give you away to him altogether.

Norman suspected him of trying to steal his own wife's property! Was he worried about the bond, the bond that would go to Frieda? My God, he'd like to punch Norman in the nose! But there was no time. Tomorrow the movers were coming, he wouldn't be able to go back to Norman's. How could he go to Florida without the package? Ah! Bella would help him.

You and Rosen were in the kitchen when I arrived. When Rosen saw me his expression was as if something unsavory had met his eyes. My experience with Norman sort of clipped my wings. It stuck in my throat and I couldn't say anything about it. In a subdued voice I explained that I needed someone to come to my apartment tomorrow when the movers will come. Would Bella please come?

Well, Rosen immediately objected. Bella has to go to Goldens Bridge, Bella has no time. I tried to plead my case, but Rosen was adamant. And, you, Bella, were silent. But then you turned to me and looked in my face. You said you will be in my apartment tomorrow morning. The heaviness in my heart lifted.

Rosen was angry. When I said good-bye he turned away and did not answer. Surely it was the first time in recorded history that a man did not offer a handshake and good wishes to a brother-in-law going off to a new life.

The next day Ben once again took the subway to Norman's. When he got there, Norman was shooting the breeze with a couple of men. Norman noticed Ben's arrival. He continued his conversation. Ben waited. Five minutes. Ten minutes. The worm turned. *I want that package! Give me that package!*

All right, all right, said Norman. Here!

Is everything in there?

Yes, yes.

But everything wasn't. The bond, which Frieda was to inherit at Lily's death, was missing. This strange bird of a brother-in-law wasn't to be trusted. (Of course the whole thing was moot anyway; Lily outlived Frieda by many years.)

—

In Miami, Ben told Lily what had happened.

"Forget about it," Lily said. "Norman didn't mean anything."

Ben wrote to Bella and told her everything.

"Norman didn't mean anything," Bella wrote back.

Family waters closed over the incident.

—

Lily and Ben lived in Miami for the rest of their lives. They ran a boardinghouse, two long bus rides from the beach. Once every few years, in summertime—because that's when the boardinghouse had empty rooms—my parents would make the drive down. I know that Norman and Frieda went down to visit, too. Everyone behaved very well. Nothing was ever mentioned about the little trouble with the package. Every other year or so, Lily would come by herself to New York.

It was quite astonishing that Lily, whose health had always been precarious, lived for such a long time. She and Ben got old in Miami. They sold the boardinghouse and bought a little two-room apartment. When she was well up in her eighties, Lily said to my mother, "My traveling days are over," and soon my mother's traveling days were over, too; she and Lily kept in touch mostly by mail. Now and then Ben would write to my mother, rehearsing old grievances.

One day we heard from my uncle Joe, who also lived in Miami. Lily and Ben were not doing well. Lily couldn't go outside without a walker, and Ben wouldn't let her use the walker outside; he was ashamed of this infirm old lady. And Lily was becoming senile. She couldn't shop or cook; there was almost no food in the house except what Ben brought. Joe described a raw chicken rotting in the refrigerator.

Well, we got busy. We got in touch with social workers; we made a large donation to a decent nursing home and got them moved in. They lived there for a number of years.

As Lily declined, Ben flourished. The nursing home was a great venue for him. He gave readings of his poetry, he read his stories, edited a little newsletter, organized concerts. He was at last a man of consequence.

I took my mother down to see Lily twice during her last years. A week after our second visit, Lily died. We said she had been waiting to see Mama one last time.

And here's something that won't surprise you. To this day I don't know whether Ben is dead or alive. The minute Lily died, we dropped him like a hot potato.

AN AMERICAN GIRL

—

In our family no one (by which I mean my mother and my aunts) was chatty on the telephone. Telephones were for terse, urgent messages: Meet me at Macy's. . . . The kid is sick. . . . The meeting is postponed. . . . My mother would even run the few blocks to the garage rather than phone my father there. In fact, it seems to me that we didn't even *have* a phone in the house until I was about twelve.

This habit of not telephoning at the drop of a hat was meant to save money; and in my family this was not only a virtue but a cause: *We are not spoiled Americans who gossip all day. We know the value of a dollar.* And, it could be added, *Don't forget the starving people of China.*

Another benefit of the sparing use of the telephone was that we got lots of mail. Anyone with information to pass along wrote, even from Brooklyn to the Bronx. *So* many letters. There was hardly a day when my mother didn't get a letter from her cousin Sylvia or my aunt Lily. Hundreds of letters. I found some of them squirreled around the house after my mother died. But although I looked particularly, I could not find even one letter from my aunt Sally. What *wouldn't* I give to read Aunt Sally's letters again!

Sally was my uncle Oscar's second wife. "An American girl" was how my mother and her sisters referred to her. This was not simply descriptive of the fact that Sally had been born in Brooklyn; no. It meant: American girls are *spoiled* girls, spoiled by America. They think they have *everything* coming to them.

How do I know this is what they meant? Because when it was what they meant, they called *me* an American girl.

(And speaking of second wives, we had another one in our family. My uncle Joe had a second wife, but he was irreproachably a widower when he came by her. Uncle Oscar was divorced.)

—

Oscar was the firstborn son—traditionally, the hope of the family. He was the eldest brother, the gentlest of uncles. Other uncles played rough and teased. Uncle Oscar took me in his lap and crooned "Brown Eyes" (in Russian). But to tell the truth, Oscar was a little . . . how to put it? Slow? Passive? Timid? Some people called him simple, meaning retarded, but that wasn't so. Oscar found the world perplexing; and, as his sisters seemed to understand everything, he put himself in their hands.

Oscar's first wife was Beatrice. Of Beatrice herself I have no memory but an old wedding photo: Oscar dressed in top hat and tails yearning over his bride; Beatrice, despite full wedding regalia, seems quite businesslike. I think Beatrice was a distant family connection from Canada, and I've heard that she was a formidably strong-minded girl. The sisters, being strong-minded girls themselves, probably thought she was just what Oscar needed. As for Beatrice, I don't know what she thought she was getting into, but I don't think she had many notions of love.

To say the marriage was not a success is to say that Mount Everest is a bump in the road. More and more frequently, as time passed, Oscar appeared at the door of one or another of his sisters to complain that Beatrice was treating him badly; close on his heels, Beatrice appeared, complaining to her sisters-in-law that their brother was a simpleton and good-for-nothing as a husband.

The sisters conferred many times on this subject. They could not bear to see Oscar so unhappy, and eventually they decided there was nothing for it but that the marriage should end. There were a few details to be worked out: the child (yes, there was a child), the store (Oscar and Beatrice ran a delicatessen), alimony.

Alimony? Who ever heard of alimony? What is this Beatrice—an American girl? We've said she can keep the store and the child! Does she think we'll let the child *starve?*

"No alimony," said the sisters to Oscar.

This piece of advice landed Oscar in alimony jail.

"Look," my father would say when we passed Bronx debtors' prison on our drive upstate. "Uncle Oscar's college!"

Beatrice was bitter about the sisters, particularly about my mother, whom she saw, no doubt correctly, as the ring-leader in the plot against her. She cut off all connection with the family. Oscar moved in with my aunt Frieda. A few years later, a matchmaker introduced him to Sally.

———

Sally. I'd never seen the like of her. Sally was square and close to the ground. Her unbelievably black hair was piled into a pompadour in front; a black net caught the fall at her shoulders. She wore bright red lipstick and rouge to match. She was lively and pure Brooklyn. You might think that Oscar would prefer the deliberately unadorned style of his sisters, but, no, he liked Sally. After their first date, he asked his sisters if he should pop the question.

"Take your pajamas!" my grandfather called as Oscar left the house for his second date.

———

Sally had never been married, and, not being a spring chicken, she had had plenty of time to look around and codify her ideas about the proper way to approach marriage. First came the engagement. The engagement, as everyone who wasn't a greenhorn knew, was announced with a ring. Not a sweet garnet in an antique setting, not a few diamond chips cunningly set, not even your simple but elegant quarter-carat solitaire. A *full* carat of diamond surrounded by appropriately sized baguettes.

This was a real jaw-dropper for the sisters. A diamond engagement ring! Who did Sally think she was? Who did she think *Oscar* was? Who did she think *they* were? You only had to glance at their hands to know what they would think about diamond rings: eight working hands, rough and thickened at the knuckle, bare of polish, innocent of any jewel, including even gold wedding bands. Who ever heard of a diamond engagement ring in this family? It costs *how much?*

But Oscar wanted to get married. And Frieda, who had her hands full not only with her own family but with my grandmother, who was also living with her, *and* Oscar, all of them in a small house in Jackson Heights, *really* wanted Oscar married.

"Let her have the ring," Frieda said.

Lily was scornful. "*Believe* me. She'll take him without a ring." My aunt Rachile was against the ring, probably because my mother was for it; Mama was for it, for Frieda's sake; and that, together with Oscar's plea, tipped the balance. I was thrilled. I couldn't wait to see this ring. I was certainly going to have one when my time came. Didn't they call me an American girl?

———

Whether from Brooklyn, where they first lived, or later, from Miami, Sally kept in close touch with her sisters-in-law. She was a brilliant correspondent: Nothing came between her and the immediate moment. She wrote as she spoke, a mile a minute, untroubled by the rules of punctuation or an internal censor. And like all great writers, she had her subject—in this case, the social activities of her family, and how much they cost.

Bessie married off her daughter Sandra last Sunday it was a grand affair, Sandra's dress was white satin with seed pearls on the bodice and Bessie told me it cost $132.65 wholesale if they had bought retail it would have been $322.98. She didn't have a train which was really a shame because it would have been another $40 but Bessie said Sandra might anyway want to dye the dress and wear it on another occasion and then they would have to cut the train off so it wasn't worth it. I have to say that Sandra looked very nice even so. Before the ceremony they had appetizers a very nice spread with whitefish, and Nova, they paid $3.95 a person, after the ceremony we sat down to a regular dinner, with roast beef or chicken, seltzer and sodas, schnapps, all you wanted $5.95 a person. Sandra's going away suit was pale blue, which she wore with matching shoes, very nice, $35 but I think beige would have been better. I wore my green silk, which I paid for $48.50 in Klein's which it's worth it because I get a lot of wear from it. Oscar wanted to

wear his brown suit but I told him blue was better and for
once he listened and we bought him a blue suit very dark
$60 but he'll have it for a long time and if he ever needs a
black suit he can wear it instead.

This is a reconstitution from memory, a shadow of the
real thing. Sally's letters were treasured in our family, read
aloud, sent to relatives in distant places, with instructions to
be sent on to other relatives. Oh, how we laughed as my
mother read them! The four sisters, sitting around the
kitchen table, laughing and laughing; Mama laughing so
hard she couldn't get the words out. I'd say Sally gave good
value.

—

In due time, Sally and Oscar retired to Miami.

"Retired from *what?*" my father wanted to know.

They lived out their final years in a single room in one of
those little run-down hotels on the Beach, in company with
other old people who'd managed to save a few dollars. Early-
bird specials, doggie bags, cronies on the beach, organized
activities—it was, I think, a pleasant life. My uncle Joe
moved to Miami Beach, and my aunt Lily lived a bus ride
away. Oscar looked very natty when we saw him, dressed by
Sally in a straw hat, a nice clean shirt, and plaid pants that
belted above his belly. Sally's hair remained as unbelievably

black as ever, her lips and cheeks as brightly red. She took up folk dancing, for which she had a wardrobe of peasant blouses with alarming décolletage. How her diamond ring sparkled as she do-si-doed!

———

A few years ago I pinned a cartoon to my bulletin board: A man and a woman are driving through the countryside. They approach a road marker that reads FEAR NO EVIL. The woman says, *"We made good time. We're already in the valley of the shadow of death."*

Those old people, my family, my uncle Oscar and aunt Sally, my uncle Joe, my aunt Lily and her husband Ben— they weren't going to be able to hold on much longer. Of course they had one foot in the grave, but they were also in trouble, demographically speaking.

Have you been to Miami Beach recently? Just as my old folks were dying off, their havens were being discovered. Who could have guessed that their seedy little hotels were Art Deco treasures? A little renovation here and there, a neon sign, some pink and turquoise paint; they turned out to be just the ticket for a lifestyle. If *Sally* was an American girl, who were *these* people?

But you know what I still wonder about? Who got Sally's ring?

LIKE GODS

—

We read the letters of the dead like
  helpless gods,
yet gods for all that, since we know
  the dates to come . . .
                    —Wisława Szymborska

February 25, 1958

Dear Miss Thornbury:

Your assignment asking your students to
tell you "Why am I taking up typing?" appears to be a simple one. The answer is not

simple. It becomes even more difficult to write about it when one remembers your remark that we needn't tell anything of a personal nature. The reasons which prompted me at this time to try to learn typing is personal and complex.

It is true that since my daughter's marriage we have to chase after her every time my husband needs to do some typing. But it would be telling only some of the truth if I was to stop right here: the need for typing in my husband's business amounts to a couple of letters a year. Besides, our daughter lives in our vicinity and has been willing to type these letters for her father.

Once or twice in the past, I toyed with the idea of trying my hand at a typewriter, but there was always a fear that I will never learn. There has always been talk about high school kids who learn quickly, and acquire speed in no time. So I used to take refuge in the belief that there are more important things to do—leaving typing to the young.

Last May—to be exact, on the 23rd—something occurred which shook my world to its very depth. A sister of mine with whom I enjoyed an unusually good relationship, was hit by an out-of-control automobile while waiting with another friend for me to keep a luncheon appointment. Her life came to an end that day; my life became some-what distorted: it felt as though the bottom had dropped out of my world. One resolution after another to become realistic about the situation would depart in great haste—leaving me in great distress.

"Develop new relationships, develop new interests," wise friends were advising me in those trying days, which were long and many. As weeks turned into months, I gradually began to realize that I was doing my sister no good by indulging in self-pity, so I began to explore possibilities of busying myself in the hope that little time would remain for brooding and reciting the events of that fateful afternoon again and again.

When Personal Typing given at the "Y" in the afternoons, came to my attention, I felt that this course would meet my needs. Little did I suspect then—two months ago—that I would find the work fascinating and even intriguing. It presented a challenge to me. At first I was frightened and was inclined more than once to drop the course. But this is where you, Miss Thornbury, come in! Always, some-how at a psychological moment, I would hear you saying: "Class, don't aim at a perfect paper," . . . or that very timely encouraging remark "Class, don't get discouraged."

I have also been admiring your resourcefulness at being able to teach a large class and find time for individual instruction. In short, with your aid, I learned that typing is a many-folded skill. It means not only learning the *keyboard*, but various techniques of the machine; one also improves his vocabulary, spelling and the division of words.

In my case typing proved to be therapy in the sense that I gained time to make if not peace, then some kind of a truce with a situation which is irrevocable and therefore not solvable. Last but surely not least, I fear no more "those high school kids." They constitute no threat to my security any longer. At times I feel as "accomplished" as Eliza Doolittle from *My Fair Lady*. She did it—and so did I!

Gratefully,

B. Rosen

November 17, 1998

Dear Ms. Thornbury,

I came across the above letter a few months ago and have been wondering what you thought when you read it. Did you realize at once that it was the work of the quiet, sixty-ish woman who sat in the last row of your class? You checked the typing for accuracy, of course; I see that there were a few mistakes, but on the whole I'd say your pupil reflects credit on you. What about grammar? Surely you noted that the syntax was not that of a native English speaker; but the writer had mastered English pretty well, don't you think? And the style? Full marks for eloquence! And I can assure you that the flattery was sincere. But, Ms. Thornbury, *what* did you think when you suddenly came upon that *cri de coeur?*

I am, of course, the daughter referred to in paragraph two and I did, indeed, do my father's bits of typing: "Dear Mr. Brown; your bill is two months past due. This state of affairs cannot continue . . ."

I imagine, Ms. Thornbury, that you were a woman of some sensibility, perhaps a retired teacher of English still wishing to be active. Your evident education and refinement inspired my mother to make you her confidante. Or it may simply be that, with her fingers placed correctly on the keyboard, she could not help pressing those keys that expressed her heart. Whatever the case, I would like to do as my mother did and take you into my confidence.

As my mother mentioned, I was married the year before she entered your class. My marriage lasted only two years and some months longer; those years seemed like a dream to me then, and so they do now.

But such odd things stay in the mind. For instance, my new mother-in-law asked me to call her Mother White.

She was a Christian Scientist. She looked just like Spring Byington. I can see her now in her dainty frocks chirping about "error." I mean no disrespect to Christians, Ms. Thornbury, but they do let it be known that it's better to give, etc. Mother White (*never* did I bring myself to utter those words) invited me to her basement to see all the furniture she had no use for; really great stuff. Oh, I said, what a pretty bureau! And that dry sink! Sofas and wing chairs— she had everything. And weren't her son and I about to set up housekeeping? So *why* did she bring me down there if she wasn't going to offer us a single blessed stick of furniture? And *why*, with all that has followed, to say nothing of all the furniture that has passed through my life, is that something that still gets my goat?

Another thing is that my mother and I went shopping for my wedding dress. She, believing that a girl only gets married once, agreed to bypass Macy's and S. Klein on the Square and head straight to Fifth Avenue. We made the round of Saks, Lord & Taylor, and Bergdorf's. (She grew timid in the presence of an elegant saleswoman.) At De Pinna's (gone for many years) we found a pale gray taffeta dress, ballerina-length, with leg-o'-mutton sleeves and a scooped neckline. We went for it, despite the seventy-five-dollar price tag. We also ordered shoes dyed to match.

My uncle Georgie, who was a caterer, supplied the food for our wedding supper.

"You want two tiers or three?" he asked me about the cake.

"Two," I answered.

Georgie said to my mother, "We'll give her three."

And here, Ms. Thornbury, let me tell you something I never told my mother. On the very night of my wedding—it was a February night, during a winter thaw—I dreamed I was trying to remove my ring (intertwined strands of three colors of gold, bought in a shop called Wedding Rings, Inc., on Eighth Street). I pulled at the ring until my finger was red and swollen. It wouldn't come off.

In the morning (we honeymooned in Jamaica) depression took hold of me. I told myself it was only delayed wedding jitters. After all, for three years I had been desperately in love with this man. I'd chased him, I'd spied on him, I'd waited in the dark outside his house to see him bring home other girls. Finally I'd landed him.

When we met, I was not much more than eighteen, he was ten years older, a man of the world. For three years he led me, as they say, a merry dance. I lost my innocence with him. Not sexual innocence, Ms. Thornbury—young as I was, I had already lost that—but worldly innocence.

You, of course, know nothing of our family history, Ms. Thornbury, but you may take it as given that although I longed for frivolity (never even having heard the word), my worldview in no way allowed for lightness of character: "Not a serious person," is what my mother would have said of someone like me. I was given to understand that the world was a deadly serious place: The forces of history ran the show; class was arraigned against class for the final conflict, the light of the future against the dark of reaction. Some years earlier I had taken a step away from our peculiar family orthodoxy. And now, casually, as if it were a simple elaboration of my life, I stepped further, and gaily, with a stranger, into taxis and French restaurants, into theaters and even nightclubs, into a sailboat! You can imagine the effect on a girl like me, a girl of two minds. We both paid for that, my husband and I, but he paid more.

So now we come to the pivotal moment, Ms. Thornbury, the one that brought my mother to your class in Personal Typing. On May 23, 1957, she called me. It was late in the morning, maybe eleven or so. My mother didn't call very often. She didn't like to "intrude," as she often said. But should I let a week go by without calling her, she would take her courage in her hands.

"Darling," she said. "I'll be in the neighborhood later. Are you going to be home?"

I was always home. I didn't make the bed until around noon. After that maybe I'd get dressed—maybe. The hours somehow passed, one by one, until, thank God, it was time to cook dinner.

"I baked a chicken," my mother said. "You know Daddy doesn't like chicken."

She had to have an offering. Just to see me. Oh, if I could, I would go down on my knees to her . . . !

Then she said, "I have to go now. I'm late. I'm meeting Frieda and Rose for lunch."

Frieda and Rose. What was the *matter* with those women, standing *outside* the restaurant waiting for my mother? I'd learned *something* from my new life. I could have told them: Ladies go *into* the restaurant. They allow the waiter to seat them—they even order a drink as they wait for their companions. But no! Like greenhorns, Frieda and Rose stood in front of the plate-glass window, looking up and down the street for my mother, until the car smashed into them. And she, when she got there, and for years and years, and maybe until the moment of her death, *knew* it was her fault.

I was dressed at two o'clock when my cousin Sylvia called. "There's been an accident," she said.

"Mama!" I said.

"No, no. Frieda."

Until I came across my mother's letter to you, I had no idea of your existence in her life, Ms. Thornbury. I would like to report to you that for a number of years, my mother continued to use the skills you taught her. Practice did not much improve her; she was never a very good typist, but she was so proud of being able to do the thing at all. And, as you will have gathered, my husband and I divorced, with great bitterness on his side, and on mine a mixture of relief and fear. These days I often think of him with regret.

In time, my mother's typewriter broke down beyond repair. She never got a new one, and I resumed typing my father's correspondence: "Dear Mr. Smith, I have been very patient but your rent is now three months overdue. If this state of affairs continues I will be forced to take steps. . . ." After 1992, there was no further need for such typing.

GOOD-FOR-NOTHING

—

In June, at the end of my sophomore year, I dropped out of Hunter College.

"Why, darling? Tell me why," my mother said to me.

"What did you expect?" my father said to her.

He was right; she should have known she hadn't raised a scholar. All varieties of mathematics sent me into a tailspin. My ear for foreign languages was as bad as my ear for music. I had some hopes for biology until they handed me a frog and a scalpel. And those papers my English teacher had liked so much? They'd been written by my ex-boyfriend—ex-fiancé, actually.

Oh yes, I was seventeen and already I had a broken engagement on my record. That accounted for some of the bitterness behind Daddy's *What did you expect?* The question had wide application in the realm of projects undertaken and abandoned. Like dancing lessons. Like design school. Like an engagement, a quite promising engagement, to a law school graduate, complete with a ring (small pearl, *pace* Aunt Sally), a party, the meeting of prospective in-laws. And then—boom! All over. He saw what he was getting: a sullen, never-satisfied-no-matter-what-he-did baby brat. But he'd already written some of my English papers.

"Go ahead, see what it's like to earn a living," Daddy said. He was struck by another thought: "Who'd hire a good-for-nothing like you, anyway?"

That summer, the summer I was eighteen, I got a job at an insurance company on William Street. Of course I got it under false pretenses.

Insurance. On the first floor of the vast enterprise that was the Continental Casualty Company there were no of-

fices, only desks. Gray metal desk after desk after desk; a
battalion of desks, each manned by a policy writer or an underwriter.

You may think that "policy writer" is simply another
name for "underwriter." That shows how little you know.
The telling difference, in those days, was that the underwrit-
ers were guys and the policy writers were girls. The under-
writers were the bosses of the policy writers. They spent
most of their time on the phone selling policies: The underwriter got to lean way back in his chair, he could put his feet
on the desk, he told jokes to his customers, he laughed and
snickered.

When his work was done, the underwriter got up from his
desk and walked over to a policy writer. He told her which
policy he had just sold. The policy writer then plucked the
appropriate policy form from stacks of such forms on her
desk. You've seen this kind of document: dozens and dozens
of paragraphs of boilerplate broken by blank spaces. The job
of the policy writer was to fill in the blank spaces.

All day, from nine to five, I sat hunched miserably over my
typewriter, clicking the roller past line after line of boilerplate, trying to adjust the spacing carefully when I reached
the blank spaces, *hoping* I could fit the provision into the
space, *praying* not to make a mistake, because if I did, I'd

have to take a new form and start all over again. Oh, and did I mention the three carbon copies that had to be made? Most of the girls were pros; their wastebaskets were empty. *My* wastebasket was filled to overflowing with ruined forms, which, when no one was looking, I'd stuff in my bag to sneak out to the ladies' room to throw away. Everyone knew my days were numbered.

So this was what it was like to earn a living. As soon as I sat down at my desk in the morning, I'd start looking at the clock. I thought it was like being in hell. On the other hand, if the Catholic God was the true God, it must have been like being in heaven.

Insurance business was Catholic business, at least on this low rung: Sullivans, O'Learys, Albaneses, Marinos. The guys were Irish; the girls, Italian—or so I remember it. The girls lived on Staten Island and in Brooklyn; the guys lived in Washington Heights and the Bronx.

All the girls were engaged or about to be engaged. We girls were always going to lunch to celebrate someone's engagement. During the two ten-minute morning breaks, girls would gather in the ladies' room to show off engagement rings. Photos of fiancés were produced and admired. Serious discussions of wedding dresses and bridesmaids' dresses took place; likewise of living room sets and bedroom drapes. The approaching wedding was the focus of all attention, the future so settled that mention of it was hardly necessary. Nothing troubled my colleagues except a few intriguing questions: premarital sex ("If I really loved him . . .") and contraception . . . whether? (most said never!) in what circumstances? what kind?

After her wedding, a girl would live in the neighborhood where she had grown up, near her parents and aunts and uncles and cousins. She would go on working for a few months or a year, until the first baby came, and then there would be more babies. These girls were so happy. Happy in this moment of freedom from domestic responsibility, working and saving money for the future; happy that they had secured the future; happy in the approval of their families; very busily happy in planning for the ultimate event. I'd never seen such pure, unclouded happiness. I knew it wasn't for me, but I was envious.

And I *liked* being included in the talk about dresses and furniture and sex. I liked office conviviality, the teasing, the gossip, the flirting (engaged or not, there was a lot of policy writer–underwriter flirting). I myself flirted with a guy named Jerry Sullivan. He happened not to be married. (Most of the guys were.) We never actually went on a date, Jerry and I; the guys always went out in a group, but we necked in dark corners.

And who did they think *I* was, to let me in on all this? Because even though I thought I'd fooled them, they knew I was from another planet.

I told you I'd taken the job under false pretenses. It was just a little thing I did, hardly anything at all. I'd stopped thinking about it even; in fact you could say I'd forgotten that on my job application I'd moved the third letter of my last name four spaces to the alphabetic right. Until the day Jerry Sullivan said to me, "You've got a call on my line. It's your mother."

The full implications of this hit me at once. I almost fainted. I'd *told* my mother that she couldn't reach me, I'd *told* her I had no phone on my desk. Yet here she was; she'd tracked me down. She *knew!*

"Are you sure it's for me?" I asked Jerry.

"Oh yeah, it's for you. She asked for Dorothy Rowen."

Jerry Sullivan smiled.

———

A few years later I was married, with a new name, a new life. While my mother took typing lessons to ease her grief, I went skiing and sailing. I went dining and drinking with my husband and our friends. I was very depressed. How perverse! Then I got pregnant.

But why *not* have a baby? Bob, that was my husband's name, wanted a baby. And what else was I going to do? I had no education, no skills, no concrete ambitions, only insistent, inchoate longings, and the above-mentioned depression. I'd wake up one morning and think: Okay, I'll have a baby, that will settle everything. The next morning: No, if I have a baby, nothing else will *ever* happen. On a day when I thought I would, we told my parents.

Oh, they were thrilled! My father said, "Dots, you want a house?" He was going to buy us a brownstone in the Village! Something about that decided me. No. No baby. Think it was spite?

Bob wasn't happy, but he said it was up to me. It was illegal, of course, but I had the name of a doctor, a good doctor, a European doctor, very skilled, very gentle. In those days these doctors were precious gold, their names whispered from ear to ear, written down on small pieces of paper, carried in the secret compartments of wallets. Skilled as they were, the best of these doctors hurt you. They couldn't use anesthetics, because you had to be able to walk out of the office pretty soon afterwards, and you were warned not to scream. The next day I stayed in bed and called my parents. Miscarriage, I said.

"Oh, darling, don't worry," my mother said. "You know, I had a miscarriage, but afterwards I had you."

———

For months after that I dreamed about babies. Dreams are boring, I know. I always skip them in books. But I'm going to tell you this one because I haven't forgotten it in all these years.

A very dark night. I'm walking alone on a narrow street walled by tall buildings. Not a light shows anywhere. It's like being in a canyon, or maybe the financial district. Then, at the very top of a building, I see a lighted window. I enter the building and start climbing the stairs. I climb many flights until I come to the top floor. I open a door. In a bare room lit by a single unshaded bulb is Camille, a girl I recognize from the insurance company. She's holding a baby. It has red hair, like my husband's hair. As I stand there, the baby falls from her arms and hits its head on the floor. It's dead. I'm horrified. But then I think, Oh well; it's a good thing I had two of them; I still have the boy.

"The kid's on the phone," my mother called to my father. "She has good news."

My father picks up the phone. "You're pregnant?" he says.

No. I wasn't calling to say I was pregnant, just that I'd gotten a good job. He wanted his grandchild. Who could blame him? That was what I was good for.

In fact I had been pregnant again, and again I'd wavered. Did I think I could keep my options open forever? Did I think I could still decide to be a ballerina? In the end I went back to the same doctor, but he wasn't doing abortions anymore. He thought the police were on to him. He gave me the name of another doctor.

I left his office and went home. At that time I lived in Brooklyn Heights with my second husband. Probably I stopped to do some shopping on the way home.

The next morning I went to work at my office, which was on Madison Avenue and Sixtieth Street. After work I met my husband and we went downtown to have dinner at John's Restaurant on East Twelfth Street. The next morning I went to work again. I'm not just marking time here; there's a reason I mention these mundane details. You'll see.

On the third day after my visit to the doctor's office, my husband and I took a subway, and a bus, to Fourteenth Street and Avenue B. It was a dark night and quite cold. We waited on the southwest corner of Fourteenth and B for twenty minutes or so. Eventually a man approached us. We identified ourselves and gave him some money. He led us to a nearby building and into a doctor's office, where I had an abortion. This was quite an unpleasant experience, but that's beside the point. We went right home after that. I took a week off work. A month, or even two months later, at six o'clock in the morning, we were awakened by a great banging at the door.

Police! Open up!

Now you see why I had to list all those long-ago perambulations. I'd been followed for three days—from the moment I left the first doctor's office. We'd had the bad luck to coincide with one of the periodic crackdowns on abortion which some assistant district attorney thought to ride to political office. (Years later I came out of my loft on the Bowery to the amazing spectacle of sanitation workers sweeping the street. "*What* are you *doing?*" I asked a sweeper. He inclined his head toward the far side of the Bowery. I saw the news cameras. It was an election year. "Bye-bye," said the street sweeper. "You won't see us here again.")

I really was just marking time there. Okay, here goes.

On that morning, in my little apartment on Orange Street, three big police officers filled my pretty living room. They flashed some piece of paper and actually said, "We're going downtown."

My brain was off-duty. If there was a Constitution, I didn't remember it. My husband said, "She's not going with you. She'll come later, with a lawyer."

Later, with a lawyer, I went downtown, to the office of,

let's say it was a Miss Connolly, who was an assistant D.A. Miss Connolly laid it out for me: We know everything, she said. We have photos of you entering and leaving the buildings where these *doctors* conducted their *business* (said with an accent of disgust). And, also, she said, we have ten women prepared to identify these *doctors* and testify as to their activities.

She spread an array of photographs out on her desk.

"Look at these!"

I looked. I recognized my nice doctors. Criminals, every one.

Miss Connolly said, Your lawyer will advise you that unless you testify before the grand jury, you will be arrested.

I turned to my lawyer. He shrugged. Nodded.

I made a feeble protest. "Why do you need me? You have ten other women."

Miss Connolly laughed.

In my defense, I might mention here that my husband had two young daughters and urged me to avoid publicity. That would be true enough. But let's be frank: I was afraid of jail, but more than that, *terrified* that *my* father would find out what I had done.

You don't know what you're made of until push comes to shove. Isn't that right, Daddy?

I don't tell this story very often.

In June, at the end of my sophomore year, I dropped out of Hunter College. That summer I thumbed my way across the country. I stopped off at a lumber camp in northern Montana, where I waitressed for a month, then crossed the Cascades into Washington and headed down the coast to San Francisco. It was the Summer of Love. I hung out with the Diggers in the Haight and went on the road with the Grateful Dead. After a few months of communal life I grew restless, so I took passage on a freighter bound for the South Seas. In Tahiti I was courted by a handsome prince, but I soon tired of the indolent life of the islands and took up my travels once more. Wherever I went, success and happiness awaited me. In Barcelona I studied flamenco and was celebrated as a prodigy of that art. In Vienna, where I studied opera, I became known far and wide for my talent and beauty. Riches and love were showered on me. I married a famous and wealthy left-wing writer, who had fought with the French Resistance. Together, we founded a journal to disseminate our ideas. It became very successful, read by influential people all over the world. Two perfect children, a boy and a girl, were born to us. After many years abroad I longed to see my parents again, so we flew to New York—

first class, and why not? At the airport my mother and father embraced us with tears of happiness. When their eyes fell upon their beautiful grandchildren, they almost fainted with joy.

At last they were speechless.

HOW I BECAME A WRITER

—

"Do you call this serious work, darling," my mother said.

It wasn't a question.

I knew where she was coming from. I came from there myself.

—

In fact, I had been floundering. But it wasn't as if I'd just been lying around all day. I had jobs. Lots of jobs, dozens of jobs, one right after the other. I'd been a salesgirl at Macy's, been in the typing pool of an insurance company, file clerk in an advertising agency, assistant to an assistant of a television producer. Receptionist was one of my frequent occupations.

So I didn't need Mama to tell me there was a problem. She, of course, had her own ideas. Long ago, by way of piano lessons, she made it clear that she intended me to be "accomplished." ("Someday you'll thank me, darling.") For the future, she was in favor of the Law (in the interests of the downtrodden), Social Work, Teaching at the very least; not to mention the Struggle for a Better World.

Myself, I had a distinct lack of ideas, negative ideas if you like. Not the Law, not Social Work, definitely not Teaching. As for the Struggle, it was just as well for It that it proceed without me. Not that It wasn't in the back of my mind *all* the time; I knew this because everything else the world offered seemed beside the point, and every moment of every day, the sense of a great mission refused rang in my head like tinnitus.

So, given the circumstances, you can see the problem: how to reconcile the high seriousness of "accomplishment," and of fighting for social and economic justice, with my evidently selfish and frivolous nature.

Mama said to take an aptitude test. I scored high on love of animals. Veterinarian? Why not? I would be called "Dr." And surely the welfare of animals was part of the struggle for a better world. But wait. I was forgetting something: Didn't I drop Biology 101 the moment I was handed the frog and scalpel? Absolutely nothing occurred to me at that moment except to register at yet another employment agency.

The ladies who ran Career Blazers were easy. They didn't seem to mind that I couldn't *do* anything, could hardly type, could not take shorthand beyond *if u cn rd th u cn gt a gd jb*. And they didn't laugh out loud when I said I wanted a Creative Job or a Job Helping People. They kept getting me the same sorts of jobs I'd been getting by myself, and I kept quitting or being fired. And because they didn't throw up their hands, I kept coming back to them. Finally they did roll their eyes; but instead of saying, Go away and learn to *do* something! they said, Well, you can work for us. And they didn't even charge me a fee.

So for a while I answered phones at Career Blazers, taking listings for jobs on offer; if a job seemed interesting, I got first crack at the interview. And one day I answered a call for the job of my life.

"I have just the candidate for you," I said. "She'll be at your office in an hour."

That was how I came to be a writer. And this is the lead paragraph of the first thing I ever wrote: *Steve McQueen drove his motorcycle through the rain-slicked streets of the Village and skidded to a stop in front of Louie's Bar. He could imagine his friends inside, laughing, smoking, drinking beer. How could he face them?*

I was a natural! So I said, "Mama. I'm going to be a writer!" She glanced at the covers of *Screen Stars* and *Movie World,* and *that's* when she said, "Do you call this serious work, darling."

—

Whatever. I began work at Magazine Management Company, where magazines were produced the way Detroit produced cars. I worked on the fan-magazine line. On the other side of a four-foot partition was the romance line. Across a corridor was the men's line. Also, there was a comic-book line.

All these "books," as I learned to call them, were the property of Mr. Goodman (no first-name bonhomie with him), who was a skinflint and something of a sadist. He maintained authority by displays of rage, and by humiliating his editors; he also had the sadist's trick of sometimes being really nice.

For a pittance (eighty dollars a week to start), Mr. Goodman hired writers with lots of talent and no money, or writers with less talent and even less money. He collected has-beens and soon-to-bes; the desperate, the bitter, the hopeful, the alcoholic, the extremely eccentric, the flotsam of society. Nothing in my experience had prepared me for such interesting colleagues. Neither was I prepared for hilarity on the job.

Such as the snowy winter night when four or five guys—editors, writers—went to Central Park. Once in the park, an editor put on snowshoes and made footprints in the snow. An assistant took pictures as a writer dashed into nearby bushes. In the resulting photograph you could just make out an ominous blurred figure obscured by brush and the large footprints the running creature left behind. The next cover of *Stag* features the headline: BIGFOOT CAPTURED ON FILM! and the story, certified to be true, tells of a brave adventurer who trekked the Himalayas in search of the legendary being.

Because we were all so poorly paid, we earned extra money by selling stories to other books. Several times I tried to write for a romance book. "He unbuttoned her blouse, and her breasts fell out." It wasn't just me. Writers with honest-to-God real books to their credit would turn out sentences like "Toward dusk, the river widened . . . I opened the glove compartment and in a second I was inside."

I never mastered the romance story, but by some odd

brain chemistry I had an immediate instinct for the fans. After I had read a few and written a few, I just *knew*. At last, I had a Creative Job.

———

A short tour of Magazine Management: It is, let's say, six months after I have started the job. I arrive at the office at nine o'clock. In the small reception area, I greet the switchboard operator. (My status is scarcely more exalted than hers; I relieve her at the switchboard three lunch hours a week.) Chatting up the pretty operator is tall, handsome Bruce Jay Friedman, who will be famous very soon. (Even after he publishes his novel *Stern* to critical acclaim, he does not feel free to call Mr. Goodman by his first name.)

And here, passing through the alcove that holds the heart of our operation—six large file cabinets containing every word published anywhere about every star and starlet—is short, squat Mario Puzo. He is working on a novel about the Mafia, he says, which he hopes will make him some money.

A few years ago, Mickey Spillane could be seen in these halls, and a few years after I leave, Martin Cruz Smith will put in his time. For now it is literary excitement enough to see Leicester Hemingway, Ernest's brother, pop in from time to time to collect his checks for fishing stories.

These are the famous and the near famous. But now here

is George Penty in his cubicle. He will never exactly be famous, but no one who has met him will ever forget him. Southern gentry, champion drinker; his conversation is conducted entirely in winks, nods, allusions, innuendos, ellipses. And George was brave enough to have been a labor organizer in parts of the country run by the Klan, although how the workers ever organized on his instructions is beyond me.

And, in the next cubicle, barking into the telephone, is the most exotic plant of all, Therese Pol, product of a one-night alliance between an Ohio piano teacher studying in Berlin and the German composer Paul Dessau. Poor Therese: her mother ran back home, leaving her in the Europe between the wars, farmed out with anyone who'd take her. Therese made her way: in Paris, as a lover of Lawrence Durrell, who used her as a model for Justine; as a translator of Wilhelm Reich and Dürrenmatt; as a writer of a few pieces for *The New Yorker*; as a great beauty. That was then. Now Therese is a ruin. Alcohol, barbiturates, and, it is rumored, a lobotomy. Still, her tongue is caustic; and she is possessed of a Teutonic obsession for accuracy, determined to make the fantasies published in *Hunting Adventures* conform to fact.

What is she saying on the telephone now?

"Tell me!" she demands of some bemused herpetologist. "Can a tarantula grow to thirty feet? . . . No? Well, how big *can* it grow? . . . Does it sun itself with its mate? . . ."

———

These are a few of my colleagues. Among them I will find a best friend, I will find love (many find love in this institution, if only for a week or two), even a husband (a second husband). But now to work.

Marge is my editor. She is throning it behind a glass partition. (In not many months, I will be throning it there myself.) I sit down at my desk outside her tiny office, one of the four desks reserved for writers of the fan magazines. And then, on this typical day, I begin to think about Elizabeth Taylor.

Let me make this plain. We had almost no access to the stars we wrote about. The big ones got all the publicity they wanted in real magazines. And even when, on occasion, a desperate starlet granted an interview, nothing resembling a secret was confided. Mostly we made things up.

Elizabeth Taylor's life is a gift to us. Events galore! Scandals one after the other, disasters right and left. But the events of her life, rapidly as they occur, still do not keep pace with the schedule of a bimonthly; and after I have written innumerable stories about how she has stolen Eddie Fisher—

the best friend of her late husband Mike Todd—from Debbie Reynolds (*Debbie may forget in time, but Debbie's babies will remember forever. Elizabeth Taylor is the woman who deprived them of their father, of a normal childhood. How will Liz be able to face her own children?*), and about how, not content with that, the hussy is *now* dumping Eddie for Richard Burton, is it possible to angle *another* fifteen-hundred-word piece with nothing but these same elements?

Some photographs are on my desk. Elizabeth Taylor pictured with each of her husbands. With Nicky Hilton, with Michael Wilding, with Mike Todd, with Eddie Fisher; and one taken just a few days earlier with Richard Burton. I stare at the pictures hoping for inspiration . . . and idly notice that Elizabeth's left hand appears in each picture. Various wedding rings can be seen. Interesting. I get out a magnifying glass. Whoa! Hold on! In the photograph with Burton, she's wearing what looks to be a wedding ring, but it is *not* the ring Eddie married her with. There's my story! Are LIZ AND DICK SECRETLY MARRIED? That I know the answer is no does not deter me for a moment.

Mrs. Eddie Fisher is wearing a new wedding ring these days, a thin platinum band, distinctly different from the wide gold ring Debbie's ex-husband put on her finger when they vowed eternal love. . . . In the second paragraph I switch to the tense in which, in the absence of any facts, much of what we produce is written.

As she held out her hand for Burton to slip the narrow band on her finger, the ring that held the promise that one day they would be truly wed, Liz must have thought of the past, as well as the future. How often over the years had she held out her hand in just this way? And each time, hadn't she believed that this *time was different,* this *time would be forever?*

And then I pull out her clipping file and fill out the rest of the piece with the well-known story of her life to date, documented by her own contemporary quotes: *"I adore him," Liz said, gazing at her new husband* [Nicky, Michael, Mike, Eddie]. *"We're so happy; we're going to grow old together."* The story will be illustrated with these very photographs, the telltale rings circled. If I say so myself, it is a stroke of genius, and everybody, from my editor to Mr. Goodman, agrees.

—

That's what I did from nine to five. Of course I didn't write nonstop. We had to keep the clipping files up-to-date. That meant reading all the other fan magazines and the gossip columns and scouring respectable magazines and newspapers. Whether or not what they reported was any more accurate than what we invented was of no matter. We also had to buy photographs of the stars from what are now called the paparazzi. We had to paste up the entire magazine and cut the stories to fit. We had to write cover titles, captions, and blurbs.

In this fashion Earth orbited more than three times, and long before this time had passed, I could single-handedly put out an entire magazine, from written word to layout.

Those years were full of professional excitements. Like the time Elizabeth Taylor sued all the fan magazines for several million dollars and Mr. Goodman told us we'd better change our tune. I wrote: *"The fog was thick in London that early Sunday morning. Liz clutched her mink coat tightly as she walked the half-remembered streets of her childhood."* Soon she meets a little girl who is out on her own. Liz stops to speak to her. She discovers that the child, whose name, by an odd chance, is also Elizabeth, lives in an orphanage, the orphanage of St. Agnes. In the course of the story, Liz makes a sizable gift to the orphanage (the single tiny kernel of fact that informs almost all our stories). And thus, in the course of a month, Elizabeth Taylor makes a quick switch from THE WOMAN MEN HATE TO LOVE to THE ANGEL OF ST. AGNES. As I wrote the dialogue between the big and the little Elizabeth, tears rolled down my cheeks.

Also during those years the Disney studios granted me an interview with Annette Funicello. I was not an experienced interviewer, so I followed the style of a previous editor known for shock tactics. In a telephone interview with an actor, this woman had been overheard asking, "Nick, when you go on a date, do you think the boy or the girl should be responsible for the contraception?"

"Annette," I said. "I think our readers would be interested in knowing why you had your nose fixed."

"I *didn't* have my nose fixed," Annette snarled. "I had an operation for a deviated septum." Unbidden, the title flashed through my mind: ANNETTE'S NIGHT OF HORROR: THE TERRIBLE THING THAT STOPPED HER BREATH.

And Mai Britt, a stunning blond Swedish actress, was briefly married to Sammy Davis, Jr. This marriage was a delicate matter. A number of our competitors finessed the issue with cover stories along the line of "How Will Mai and Sammy Explain Their Love to Their Children?" But hadn't I been raised in a tradition so insistent on color blindness that when you wanted, for instance, to point out the sole black person in a group of whites, you were forced to say, "He's the guy with the blue sweater and brown pants."? So, while I acknowledged that there was a social problem inherent in this mating, it was different from the one you might expect:

"I love him," said Mai Britt. "I know there are differences between us. Some people will never understand why I married a man shorter than I am."

———

When Marge left, I took my courage in both hands and went to Mr. Goodman. It needed courage, believe me. Strong men tossed back double martinis to prepare themselves for the ordeal of explaining to Mr. Goodman why sales figures were not up to par.

"Why should I give *you* the job?" said Mr. Goodman.

"Because I think I can do it."

"You *think* you can do it?"

Mr. Goodman stared at me for a long moment. "Okay. Let's see."

Things went along swimmingly for a while. I started an advice column, "Talk It Over with Nan Tyler," and vouched for Nan's reality by running a photograph of our bookkeeper at the top of the column. I hardly need to say that we wrote all the letters as well as the answers. I also sent *Movie World*'s special correspondent to Hollywood, so that she could renew her personal friendships with the stars and bring back news straight from their mouths. To document this event I had a photograph taken of myself, the editor, at my desk, shaking the switchboard operator's hand in bon voyage.

But all good things come to an end. One day a photographer brought me some pictures of Connie Stevens to choose among for a cover. I bought one for the following issue of *Screen Stars*. Connie, all flirtatious smiles, leaned back against a tree. The cover was printed, the magazine bound and shipped and, just as the issue was about to go on sale, someone noticed a carving on the tree: MARY SUCKS BLACK COCK. *You* try explaining that to Mr. Goodman.

So that was that. I didn't mind. It was time to go. I'd learned just about everything there was to learn. And I had this strange feeling. I wanted to do some serious work.

BY THE BOOK

—

I saw an ad in the paper. Bowery loft. Sunny. 1,000 sq. ft. 199/mo.

I was looking for an apartment. Two hundred a month was exactly what I'd had in mind.

—

A little-publicized aspect of happiness is being in the condition of not having to look

in the classifieds. Not for a job, not for an apartment, surely
not for love. For a number of years I'd been well situated in
Brooklyn Heights. I had a darling apartment, the whole top
floor of a very small building on Orange Street, which is
sandwiched prettily between Pineapple and Cranberry. The
house was owned by a family of Jehovah's Witnesses. They
lived on the lower two floors and always peered into the hallway when I came home. No doubt to see if I was sneaking a
man home. I was sorry to disappoint them so often.

What I still miss about that apartment is the bathroom. It
was a comparatively large room, as large as the living room.
I kept a dressing table and chair in it, and on winter Sundays
I'd get into the old claw-foot tub, which was right beside a
sunny window, and stay there reading for hours, not anwer-
ing the doorbell when the Jehovahs rang to proselytize. This
may have been why, when my lease was up, the Jehovahs gave
my apartment to their own kind. So, back to the classifieds.

By this time I was a twice-divorced woman with an extant
broken heart due to a recent romance. Plus, I was sick of my
job. I'd been working at a women's magazine—oh, let's
name it: *Redbook*—as an editor in the articles department.
If socio-porn were a category, it would describe most of these
articles. DOES ADULTERY ENHANCE MARRIAGE? A SOCIOLOGIST
SURVEYS 10,000 WOMEN. . . . OLDER MEN, YOUNGER WOMEN? A

SYMPOSIUM. (It was odd—some might say ironic, but they would be wrong—that the experts always answered these questions with a resounding affirmative. I sometimes wondered if my boss's wife had ever been scientifically surveyed; if so, did she know about her husband's young secretary, who was quite a cute little number?) Anyway, my life was definitely not going according to plan. And just what was this plan, please?

———

The reason I couldn't pay more than two hundred dollars a month for an apartment is that I was quitting my job to make my way as a freelance writer. These days, you couldn't get your overhead low enough to take the chance. These days, you'd be lucky if two hundred dollars was all you had to pay for dinner at a fashionable Bowery club. *If* you could get in. In the days I'm talking about, the Bowery was still your basic, if world-class, skid row, and the Lower East Side was where your penniless grandmother had to live when she first came to this country.

I was a little nervous about the neighborhood, so I took my friend Liz with me when I went to see the loft. We started from Bleecker Street, walking down the west side of the Bowery. It was summer. The heat was infernal. The smell of urine and vomit seemed to hang just at nostril level. We stepped over bodies, detoured around them. Here and there arms reached for us; if not for that, I'd have sworn most of the guys of the sidewalk were dead. *Can I do this?*

The building, 215 Bowery, was on the northeast corner of the Bowery and Rivington Street. We stood across the street looking at it: dark brown stone, five very tall stories high, with a cash-register store on the ground floor. The entrance was on the Bowery; the rest of the building wrapped around the corner.

"Look!" said Liz. "A doorman." ("Just drag my doorman out of the doorway," I instructed visitors for the next decade.) We crossed the street, coaxed the prone body out of the way, and climbed to the third floor. A guy opened the door. The place of my dreams. Really.

Empty, and flooded with light. Pressed-tin ceilings thirteen feet high. Seven windows, each one ten feet tall, faced south onto Rivington Street. Unobstructed, the sun poured in. Three more windows faced west across the Bowery, with a view of three doll-sized, dormered Federal houses.

At the eastern end of the loft, the previous tenant had horizontally bisected an alcove: a room-sized closet below, a sleeping platform above. Except for that, the space was open. The eye took in everything at once. I had no doubt. This was my place. I could see my life here.

Except, possibly, it could use some redecoration. The narrow plank floors had been painted black; I'd repaint in pale putty. White for the walls and ceiling. Get rid of the blackout shades. The couch goes at the far end, the table over there, the desk over here . . . I climbed the wooden ladder leading from the closet to the bedroom. The space was large enough to hold a double bed, a small chest, a chair. I could stand up if I slumped a bit.

From the south window where I intended to put my desk there was a view across Rivington Street of One Mile House, a decaying three-story bar/flophouse, built on the site of the old mile-marker from City Hall. Through all the years I looked across the street, a rag mop hung from the same third-floor window. In the early mornings, when I sat down at my desk, the sun lit up One Mile House. Every detail of shadowed windows, peeling paint, and crumbling bricks, every strand of the mop, was thrown into brilliant relief. The sight filled my window like a life-sized Hopper.

On some nights, the room across from my desk remained dark, but on many nights, a bare ceiling bulb switched on. Then I saw a scrawny old man (maybe always the same man) sitting in his underwear on a narrow metal bed. Sometimes he sat with his head in his hands, sometimes he walked around the room; from time to time he looked toward my window. In this way many a New Year's Eve passed.

———

"You're going to live *here*, darling?" my mother said.

Anybody's mother would be dubious: no real bathroom, no kitchen sink, no air-conditioning, hardly any heat, the neighborhood, the drunks, the seemingly downward social slide.

"And, darling," she said. "So much noise!"

She meant the music, piped in by loudspeaker from the Dominican social club across the street. At that particular moment, the summer's favorite happened to be playing: *I'll be thereeee / before the neeeext / teardrop faaallls* . . .

But Daddy. He was thrilled: the rent, the lack of amenities, the badly needed repairs. He liked the style. It was *his* style. He had me at his mercy.

"You need a kitchen sink," he said. "Good. I got a sink for you."

He ripped out the old hand basin, left over from the time when the place was a sewing loft, and put in an elderly kitchen sink, which he must have found by the side of a road.

"Let's see the bathroom."

Bathroom? Two narrow side-by-side doors, the original toilet stalls for the workers. (I knew the place had once been a garment shop, because some needles were still embedded between the narrow floorboards.) One door opened to the surviving toilet; the second toilet had been converted into a makeshift shower. The floors were rough concrete. Did Daddy have some tiles stashed somewhere?

He flushed the toilet. "Good enough," he said, meaning the water pressure.

He eyed the ladder to the sleeping loft. "It's *fine*, Daddy."

"We'll see," he said.

"Heat?"

There was actually one small radiator, but mainly there was the stove, a potbellied wood-burning stove.

"Ah!" he said. It made him glad. He knew what a stove needed: wood. *There* was a job without end. Over the years he brought me wood: scavenged wood from building sites, wood coated with creosote, thus adding immeasurably to the danger of a chimney fire; wood full of rusted nails that could give you tetanus if you handled it carelessly and that sounded like Fourth of July cherry bombs when it burned.

I was all set. Now what?

———

No more nine to five, no more regular paychecks—I was going to be a writer. What kind of a writer remained to be seen. For a few years I traveled around the country chasing stories: I lived in a whorehouse in Nevada for five days. Not exactly *in* the whorehouse but in a small, freezing shack out back; in their off-hours, I talked to the whores. ("What's a nice girl like you . . . ?" Will it surprise you to learn they did it for the money?) I went to California to write a story about a woman whose arms were eaten off by a bear. I went to Idaho to write about the collapse of the Teton Dam. I was on a jury that tried a murder case, and I wrote about that. I went to the Yakima Valley to write a piece about a ninety-nine-year-old woman and five very much alive generations of her female descendants. An editor asked me to expand that piece into a book, and for a couple of years I worked on that.

My darling daughter,

I have been remembering that when you wrote about Elizabeth Taylor, I said that I didn't think that a serious magazine would print the article. My dear daughter, I hurt your feelings, but I know that you have forgiven me. If you hadn't I would have been eating my heart out all these years. How ignorant I was of what it takes to "create." I should have known better . . . Daddy and I are very proud of you, even if Daddy has never mentioned it . . .

So, evidently, I wasn't a total loss. I'd written a book. Mind you, not a book I felt deeply attached to; it hadn't been *my* idea, after all, but it was a respectable book, one that made my mother, even my father, proud. (As it happened, it met the fate of many respectable books; it fell into a Black Hole. I say this with no bitterness. Bitterness comes later.) I was agreeably surprised to have produced a book. I liked the perks, among them having Mama eat her words. And it seems I was having a career. Not brilliant, but I was working steadily, meeting deadlines, seeing my words in print. No rejections, no kill fees. Not bad.

And with success came the idea that I could write *another* book. I had a subject. Doesn't every writer make use of his history? What was my history? Wasn't it History itself?

Oh, but this was getting serious. I was thinking of taking on the very story of Communism. And much more. Because how can you separate Communism from everything else going on? So, let's assume here that I'm even capable of researching and mastering so immense a body of factual material. What organizing principle would sustain such a book? It was *so* complicated, *so* many strands weaving back and forth through *so* many years, leading in *so* many directions, to *so* many actors, *so* many events. It was too much to comprehend! . . . Too complicated! . . . Impossible! . . . Out of the question! . . . I'd just forget the whole thing. Who would know that I had shirked the one piece of work that was necessary to me?

And here fate takes a hand. One summer evening, I went to a dinner party. It was a lively evening; interesting conversation took place. By dessert, I saw my way. A few days later I went to the library to see what I could find out about an obscure, murdered, Italian-born anarchist named Carlo Tresca. Not so many days after that, I proposed a biography of Carlo Tresca to a prominent and famously boyish editor at a very classy publishing house.

Terrific idea, he said. Sign here.

—

I know what you're saying now: Carlo *who?* Multitudes would say the same. Never mind.

From his birth in 1879, in the mountain village of Sulmona, in the Abruzzi, until his murder in 1943, on Fifth Avenue and Fifteenth Street, I tracked Carlo Tresca. Luck had been with me when, knowing almost nothing about him, I chose him; and luck stayed with me.

Lucky for me he was murdered: What more satisfying design for a book than a murder mystery?

Lucky for me he was a man with a gift for making friends: His friendships were deep, ranged widely, and represented every political current on the left.

Lucky for me he had a talent for making enemies—the right enemies: Mussolini was one of his very personal enemies; others embodied the rising ideologies of Communism and Fascism.

Lucky for me he was Italian: He had dealings with the Mafia, and we know how inherently interesting the Mafia is.

Lucky for me he was a womanizer: Nothing like love affairs to spice up history.

Luckiest of all, he was an anarchist. That was *exactly* the perspective I needed to see through the rousing slogans, the marching songs, through the exhortations to the proletariat (all of which had clouded my brain), and into the dark heart of Soviet Communism. Carlo Tresca was my long-deferred education in History, writ large and personal. I could hardly believe my luck!

—

I worked on research for many years. Documents had to be wrested from government agencies that seemed to exist for the very purpose of preventing me from seeing what was in their files. But I was very diligent, very persistent; by and large I got what I needed. I began with a two-drawer file cabinet; I added a four-drawer cabinet and every drawer was crammed full. You could say I became obsessed with my project, even a little mad. For one thing, I worried a *lot* about a guy in Illinois who was, I learned, also working on a biography of Tresca. Eventually I got his name. An Italian name—*not* a good sign. I dug a little deeper. His *father* had known Tresca. Oh, God; this guy had the inside track. I called the guy up.

Tresca! he said. Why are *you* doing Tresca? Do you know *anything* about the anarchist movement? Do you speak Italian, do you read Italian?

Not exactly, I said with some exaggeration.

He laughed. Oh, go right ahead then, he said. I'm almost finished; I'm working on my last chapter.

(Dear Reader, as I write so many years later, he hasn't yet finished. Not long after *I* had finished, we appeared together on a panel. I have to admit it, the guy knew his stuff. He was deeply knowledgeable. And when he had concluded his erudite remarks, he smiled at the audience and turned to me: "Dorothy," he said, "will now discuss Carlo Tresca's love life." Really! Had I made a dime, I would have cried all the way to the bank.)

Not only did I expend a lot of energy worrying about my rival, I also worried about robbery, and about fire destroying my files. I could *do* something about that: I bought a fireproof safe and kept my most important papers in it.

Now, everything I have just related is proof of the adage that the things you worry about are not the things that happen. As far as the safe was concerned, I might better have put myself in it, for now enters a real danger.

He arrives by telephone. A stranger. He's interested in my subject, he says. Can we meet and talk?

Of course. Delighted. So pleased to talk about my obscure subject. Not many are interested. And this guy turns out to be quite attractive. Soon he's giving every indication that he's interested in me as well.

Dinner? Why not? So much to talk about.

Well. After a few dinners, and the rest of it, he wonders if he can borrow some portion of my files for a paper he's giving at some academic conference having to do with an aspect of our mutual work.

Here, as they say, I hesitate visibly. *You* know how I feel about these documents. But this attractive guy seems quite annoyed by my reluctance. He speaks—almost sharply— about the obligations of collegiality and scholarly generosity. He makes reference to our burgeoning romance. He is, if he says so himself, sincerely hurt by my evident distrust.

Yes! Indeed! He walks off with a portion of my hard-won files and I never hear from him again.

—

A diversion, merely. I am inexorably on my path. Eight years after I began work, my book was finished. Then my luck really ran out.

Dear Dorothy [wrote my editor, famous worldwide for his literary discernment],

I'm sorry to have to tell you . . . don't know what to say . . . would like to help you but . . . so badly written that . . . unpublishable . . . rewritten from beginning to end . . . even so, can't see how it can ever . . .

Depressed? No, not depressed. Shamed. Paralyzed with shame. *Avoid shame,* reads the inscription on a gravestone somewhere in England. *People must not be humiliated,* says Chekhov. I was *so* ashamed that I could not pick up my clothes at the dry cleaner. How could I? The dry cleaner had the idea that I was a writer. Walk the dog? Some other dog walker might ask how my book was going. (Eight years of walking the dog is a long time; you have to say something.) See friends? Go to a party? I could barely buy a quart of milk.

At last, after two long years in this wilderness, a university press took my manuscript.

Reviews began to appear:

A first-class book . . . a perfect detective story . . . brings back a whole period in American life. . . . Important but neglected figure. . . . Exciting. . . . Absorbing. . . . Fine in-

vestigative work . . . chilling historical insights. . . . Im-
mensely interesting . . .

On the Thursday night before the Sunday when a full-page, glowing (if I may say so) review of my book would appear in the *Times Book Review,* I went to somebody else's book party. (See how much better I was feeling?) In the lobby, boarding the elevator with me, was my erstwhile editor. I trembled; or shivered. I positioned myself at his side. Shoulder to shoulder we stood, facing front.

"Bob," I said to the elevator door. "What a *terrible* letter you wrote me."

"Really?" he said. Behind his large horn-rimmed glasses, I could imagine his eyebrows lifting in surprise. "I'm so *surprised* to hear you say so," he said. "Why, I have drawerfuls of letters from writers thanking me for my tact."

"I don't think so," I said. "Just possibly, you have *drawersful.*"

And what was that? A pinprick when I longed for a sledgehammer. Pathetic, right? But, and maybe you'll agree, a writerly weapon nevertheless.

SOCIAL HISTORY

—

I happened to be at home when Rose phoned. I saw my mother pick up the phone, listen. I saw her clap her hand to her mouth. I heard her say angrily, "We begged her to move. *Didn't* we beg her? She was so *stubborn!*"

Clara Isserman, widow of my father's best friend, had been found dead, found murdered, in the apartment where she had lived for almost thirty years.

I hadn't been in that building or neighborhood since I was a kid, but I remembered it pretty well. It was in the East Bronx. A lot of our friends and relatives lived in the East Bronx. You got to the East Bronx on the El, riding above an interminable shadowed and light-slashed street. Looking out the window of the train, you saw fragments of life in the apartment windows at eye level: dirty, limp curtains flapping, potted plants dying, forty-watt bulbs hanging from ceiling cords. Sometimes you looked right into the face of a tenant leaning from a sixth-floor window.

Really poor people lived in the buildings that lined the El. On either side of the tracks the more advantaged lived, on street after street of soot-stained five-, six-, seven-story tenements. These streets stretched as far as you could see: the concrete sidewalks, the stone buildings; I don't remember any trees. There weren't many sights to lift the spirits in the East Bronx, but in those days the housing was still intact, the rents were cheap, and landlords were required to paint your apartment every three years. In those days, there was work in small manufacturing companies nearby. In those days, there was a working class, and this was one of their neighborhoods. We lived in a neighborhood very much like it in Washington Heights.

The Issermans lived several blocks from the El, in a building at the top of a hilly street. They had a view that was almost a vista of vacant weed- and brush-filled lots. On long-ago Sundays, we often went to visit Clara and Yitzak and, in time, their daughter, Toby.

———

The men talk in the living room, and I follow my mother and Clara into the kitchen. In a high-pitched singsong (a soprano that is heartbreakingly beautiful when I hear her sing Yiddish songs on the radio), Clara lists her husband's derelictions. *He doesn't care for me . . . he doesn't do what he promises . . . he gives too much money to the Cause . . . he spoils the child . . . he turns the child against me . . .* My mother listens patiently, protesting from time to time, but Clara is unstoppable. She is filled with grievance. *You think he's so good, you don't know him!*

But he *is* good. He is slight, bald, and, as far as I can tell, deeply sweet in his nature. He is a housepainter by trade, a decorator and builder when he gets the chance. He is my father's best friend. They are boyhood friends. They are *landsmen*. They even share a name: Yitzak. Yitzak Isserman is the one person who knew and loved my father in that unimaginable distant past, in that unimaginable distant place. He is the one who shows me my father:

Your grandfather was a tanner in our town. Lomazy. He was a hard man, a strict man. Very strict. Sometimes, and not so seldom, he would beat your daddy, because, to tell the truth, your daddy was a little wild. Like what? Like the trick he played on the old blind man. Well, never mind.

Your zayde made your daddy work in the tannery. It was a terrible place. Such a stink! But also Zayde wanted a rabbi in the family for the honor of it, and your daddy was supposed to study to become a rabbi. To say the least, he was no scholar, but don't say I told you. They had a lot of fights.

All of us boys dreamed of America. Your daddy was the first to go. He had courage. One day he just disappeared. I knew his plan. He took some money Zayde had hidden in the barn. And then, knowing that Zayde would send some- one to find him, he played a trick. (The truth is, he was al- ways playing tricks.) He took the train to Warsaw. From Warsaw, he sent a letter home: "Don't look for me. I'm going to Rotterdam to take the boat for America." Instead, he got on a train to Hamburg and took the ship from there.

Even so, he was almost caught. A fellow townsman recognized him on the train.

"Aren't you Yitzak Rosenbloom?"

"No," your daddy said. "I'm Yitzak Isserman." (He always thought quickly.)

"Really? Do you know that Yitzak Rosenbloom ran away from home?"

"I don't believe it!" said your daddy. "He would have told me. He's my best friend!"

The friends lost track of each other for more than a decade. Then one day, crossing one of those light-slashed streets under the El, they found each other.

"*Yitzak!*" they cried with joy.

Boyhood had passed; they were men approaching thirty, with more adventures behind them than they would have the rest of their lives.

In a luncheonette under the El, with trains periodically drowning his words, Isserman tells his story. He had joined the Socialist Bund in Poland. After the revolution in Russia, he became active with the Communists. The authorities cracked down and he fled to Germany, where the revolution was soon expected. When the uprising failed, he was thrown in jail. And there he languished until Clara, who had been in love with him in their hometown, who had followed him to Germany despite his indifference to her, managed to get him released. She was very tenacious—you had to give her that. And also, she was musically gifted.

"So," Isserman said, "we got married."

My father remembered Clara. "So. You married her."

My father's story had its drama, too. The steerage passage from Hamburg to America, ending not in New York but in Galveston. What a place! Hot as hell! His first job: driving a horse and a wagon filled with bananas to sell to farmers on outlying farms; on the road for a week at a time, sleeping in barns when he got permission, sometimes eating nothing but bananas. I'm sure he told the story of how, one evening, with his few words of English, he asked a farmwife, "Can I sleep with you tonight?"

And after a few years in Texas, he is rescued. A train ticket to Philadelphia arrives from a friend, his one friend in America, a fellow passenger on the ship that brought them. In Philadelphia there were people who spoke his language, and factory jobs that began before dawn; beds in boardinghouses shared with someone on the night shift; onion sandwiches for lunch; $1.50 for a meal ticket that bought a week's dinners. And, yes, he had met a girl in Philadelphia. He, too, was a married man, eight years now.

No, no children (and not for another eight years). Now he was a laundryman. All day he drove a truck, picking up dirty laundry and delivering wet wash. Up the tenement stairs carrying the heavy loads of wash on his back, calling, *Wet wash! Wet wash!*

So after these long years of wandering, here they were in the Bronx, each with a best friend again.

———

Seven or eight years after I was born, Isserman and Clara had Toby. "You were their inspiration," my mother said. "Be a sister to her."

Not a chance. First of all, I liked not having a sister; second, I never liked Toby. From the first, she was a disagreeable, imperious child, her face always screwed up, about to wail, and when she began to talk she had her mother's high, complaining voice. Toby was smart, all right; she knew how to play mother against father, and she grew up willful and with no charm that I ever noticed. Isserman adored and spoiled her, Clara shrieked at both of them.

Isserman died of a heart attack when he was not much more than sixty. To everyone's consternation, my father, who never showed feeling, wept. By that time Toby must have been close to twenty. She had moved out of Ward Avenue a couple of years before, to live on the Lower East Side.

And now, without Isserman to mediate, the battles between mother and daughter grew fiercer. Toby demanded money: *It was my father's money, he wanted me to have it.* Clara withheld: *When you finish school . . . when you stop hanging around with those degenerates . . . when you start treating me with some respect.*

I would hear about this from my mother, from Rose. They'd roll their eyes despairingly: "Only in America," they'd say. For Isserman's sake, they kept in touch with Clara.

Eventually Toby moved to California. We heard that she married, then that a child had been born. So Toby was growing up, settling down; Clara sent money. But after a few years we heard of some troubles, unspecified. Clara told my mother that the grandparents were raising the child. This was the last straw; she had made it clear to Toby, she told my mother, that no more money would be forthcoming.

Clara stayed on in the apartment on Ward Avenue. She continued to sing in the Yiddish chorus, and once in a while, I heard her on WNYC, her voice as sweet and pure as ever. But she was bitter, getting old, and she was very lonely. The neighborhood had changed: With muggings and burglaries ever more common, Clara's nearby friends, like Rose, grew fearful and fled. Everyone urged Clara to move, but, as my mother said, she was stubborn.

And then she did decide to move. To California. Who else did she have in the world but Toby? And now a grandson. She began to pack up her apartment; in the lobby of her building, she put up a notice of household goods for sale.

A few days before Clara was to leave, she and Rose made a date for a farewell lunch. When Clara didn't show up, Rose telephoned. No answer that afternoon, no answer that evening, no answer the next morning. "I feared the worst," said Rose, although the worst turned out to be something she couldn't imagine. So she called the police and went with them to Clara's apartment. The door was unlocked. They found Clara in a half-filled bathtub, dressed only in a bra and panties, floating facedown. No accident, the police said.

Toby came east for the funeral. I saw her for the first time in years. She looked the same. We exchanged a few words: *How terrible . . . I'm so sorry . . . yes it was horrible . . . no the police don't have a clue.*

—

Years passed, and I thought about Clara from time to time. I thought about the manner of her death, which had so shocked everyone, but really no one had mourned her, certainly not as her husband had been mourned. She was nobody's beloved and she knew it. I thought about moments that must have redeemed her life: that long-ago day, for instance, when, having managed to get Isserman released from prison, she knew that she had won him—that day, she must have been triumphantly happy. And her music, singing would have brought elation; pregnancy, the birth of her daughter—before she knew how badly that lottery would turn out. Her last moments didn't bear thinking about at all.

Ah, but I was thinking about it; and what I thought was: Why waste good material? I had an idea that I could use Clara's life and death as an occasion for a high-class piece of social history. I could see it in *Harper's*, or *The Atlantic*: the changing demographics of a Bronx neighborhood, a once stable working-class community slipping into decay and disorder as the local economy declined and jobs fled; the population shift to black and Hispanic—all of it leading inevitably to the moment when a dark stranger knocked on Clara Isserman's door, knowing that an old, defenseless white woman had a little money from the sale of household goods.

When I called the local police precinct and said I wanted to talk to them about Clara Isserman's murder, the detective was quite accommodating. Anytime, he said. In fact, he said, I'll have a squad car meet you at the station. I did think that was a little odd.

I rode the El up to the Bronx. Not much had changed. I remembered those limp curtains and dying plants, the forty-watt bulbs, the tired faces peering from sixth-floor-walk-up windows. At the end of the line, the promised squad car waited. And in a small room, entirely filled up by three detectives, I began to ask my questions. Except it was soon evident that I was not in charge.

What was your relation to the deceased? . . . Didn't you say that she was your aunt? . . . She wasn't exactly your aunt? . . . How close are you to her daughter? . . . When were you last in touch with her? . . . Do you know her husband? . . . Do you recognize the person in this picture?

I was handed a glossy black-and-white photograph in which I recognized, *barely* recognized, Toby. Her face was bruised and swollen. Her eyes stared blankly into the lens. Printed on her chest was a series of numbers. Let me tell you, I was stunned! Evidently, Toby had a record—allegedly for selling drugs, for prostitution. For the police, it was a routine assumption that this small-time-criminal history could lead to murder. According to their scenario, it was possible that Toby, or her husband, or both of them—desperate characters—had come east to get money from Clara. They would have had a key to the apartment, and surprised a half-dressed Clara. There was a fight. Tempers flared. Clara was hit on the head. To confuse evidence, they put Clara's body in the bathtub.

I asked about the evidence. None, really. Just a vaguely re-ported sighting of a young white male in Clara's building at the requisite time. Not nearly enough to justify the expense of sending a detective to California to question Toby. Hence the hospitality of a squad car to me. Would I write to Toby and invite her to New York?

I said, No, we're not on those terms. I said, Sure, I'll let you know if I ever hear that Toby is in New York.

—

I took the El and went home. As you can imagine I was quite dejected. How in the world could I write my social history without a dark stranger?

THE LAST INDIAN

—

Yes, almost all of them were gone, and yet I saw them everywhere. *There goes another one of my dead,* I'd think as I watched an old woman hauling herself onto a kneeling bus. Struggling down the block with heavy shopping bags. In a wheelchair, pushed by a minder. Is that my daddy beetling along in his plaid loggers' cap? Uncle Oscar standing in the courtesy line at the bank? My own mama, teetering on the curb, stretching out a supplicant's hand to a stranger for balance? My aunt Lily, sitting on a bench on one of those dirty islands in the middle of Broadway traffic, raising her face for a warming ray of sun? It seems to me I didn't see my relations this often when they were alive.

—

I still had one left. My aunt Rachile was hanging on in California. I went to see her, and we spoke of family matters.

"Your mother," said my aunt Rachile. "I could tell you things about your mother."

"Maybe not today," I said.

It was mean to cut her off like that; grievances had been her life. But my mother had died only a month before and, *really*, she might have had some consideration. But, you know, Rachile had always been histrionic, half-crazed with grievance. I was heartened to see that her center still held. She was a brave girl in her way.

—

In the earliest picture I've ever seen of her, Rachile is in a family group: a passport photo, taken in 1922, in Bucharest. My grandmother and grandfather are there, only in their fifties, staring grimly into the lens. Surrounding them are four of my shockingly young aunts and uncles: Frieda, maybe twenty; Rachile and her twin brother, Joe, eighteen; I see that Berca (who will be called Georgie in America) is about ten, and that his jaw has already been deformed by an untreated infection.

The camera has caught them in extremis: six frightened, bewildered refugees. My refugees (they *are* mine; these pages are their last home) have fled Ukraine and crossed the Romanian border. Running for their lives from famine, pogroms, the Bolshevik revolution, civil war, etc. Running like hell, from history, no less.

Of course at the moment the shutter snaps, they haven't a clue how lucky they are, how much history they will be spared. They are going to America, where my grandfather, clever man, sent his older children before the war; those three—Lily, Oscar, and Bella—are absent from the photo, as is the eldest of the children, Rifka. She's the aunt who stayed behind with her husband and child. Why she stayed, I can't imagine. She'd already been raped during a pogrom. In 1942, history—which, as I was always instructed, consists of vast, inexorable forces, always progressive in tendency—will find her in Odessa, where she and her husband will be killed in the ghetto, along with fifty thousand other Jews. By Romanians, not Germans—if it matters.

———

When Rachile was born, in 1904, she was the sixth child and the fifth girl. Oscar was the only boy. You may recall that he wasn't quite living up to expectations. I need hardly say, then, that Rachile's emergence from the womb was greeted with a groan of . . . *not* joy. But, wait! My bubbe isn't finished; a few minutes later her contractions resume and out comes Joe, the second longed-for son. Poor Rachile. Twice cursed just as her life begins. Two more sons came later, but first impressions are lasting.

—

"What was Bubbe like?" I asked Rachile.

"She was a beast."

Just then I noticed a narrow copper-colored band on Rachile's finger; it left a black trace. Not gold.

"What's that?"

"Your grandmother's wedding ring."

"Can I have it?"

"What do you want it for? It was a miserable marriage."

"Tell more about Bubbe."

"What else do you want? She was beautiful. She was very clean. In summer she always dressed in white. Your grandfather adored her, but she wouldn't sleep with him. She loved her sons. Joe, she loved most of all. Me, she hated. Selfish beast!"

—

That my grandmother favored her sons was a given. In that part of the world, at that time, a son was "an egg with two yolks" (a double irony in the case of these particular twins). But she loved her older daughters. She loved my mother; *that* was gall to Rachile. And also, by the time Rachile came along, her four sisters had carved out their sisterly roles and their places in the family: Lily, the bossy one—*really* bossy; Frieda, the conciliator; Bella, the precocious one. Poor Rachile. How was she going to break into that tight circle? And let's add here that, judging by her temperament in later life, she may have been a hard child to love.

The way it worked in those days was that the girls, when they reached the age of five or six, had to take care of the latest infant. My mother was six when Rachile and Joe were born: *her* turn! But Bella lucked out. (As usual! Rachile would say bitterly.) Shortly before the twins were born, my grandmother's sister, Hannah, arrived from the nearby town of Brailov to help out. Hannah was childless.

"You have too many children," my great-aunt Hannah said to my grandmother. "Give me Bella."

My mother jumped for joy. How she had *dreaded* the prospect of taking care of the new baby. Babies!

Please, please, please! she begged.

So what happened, as Rachile saw it, was that *Bella* got to evade her duty to Rachile, *Bella* got to live in a bigger town, where she could get a better education (she *was* a prize pupil), *Bella* got to live in a household where she got all the love and attention.

And what did Rachile get? *Bupkes.* She got Lily as a care-taker, and Lily was *so* mean to her. She got no education (she never learned to write properly), no affection from her mother—just the opposite. What she did get was all the scut work in the house while the older children went to school; she got to take care of Georgie. And she finally found her role in the family—the scapegoat—and a mode of expres-sion: hysterics.

—

Rachile was no Cinderella who held her tongue. Everything spilled out. Surely, if she rehearsed her wrongs often enough, expressed them with enough feeling, placed enough blame on her persecutors, told enough people, justice would be given her. Anyone could have told her that she was taking exactly the wrong tack, but she couldn't help herself; she really couldn't. She cornered people and railed at them: *my mother! my sisters! Bella this! Lily that!*

—

But I'm getting ahead of myself. It's still 1922, and the ship carrying my refugees is just making port in New York. My father and mother have been married for two years. Oscar and Lily are still single. On the day the ship arrives, Oscar and Lily are at work, and my mother is putting the final touches on the Bronx apartment where the whole family will live. My father goes to meet the ship. He brings the refugees back to the apartment, and he's smiling. Pretty girls, he says to my mother (in English, so the pretty girls won't understand).

Except for Lily, who was never too much in the looks department, the girls, in youth, are beauties. Rachile is prettiest, after my mother. She's slight, with high cheekbones, dark hair, and hazel eyes. And she is *very* flirtatious, more so than all her sisters put together. Probably she's already given my father the business on the way from the boat to the Bronx, which would account for his smile. But if you happened to be a close observer of human behavior, you might want to be careful of Rachile. Even flirting, she's too intense for comfort; her small, tight half-smile is self-conscious; even as she seduces, and flaunts herself, she watches. And you'd better mind your manners, because the slightest sign of indifference will be quickly interpreted as a direct insult. And then you'd be in for it. Oh! such reproaches, more or less vehemently expressed.

But, remember, we are talking about a very pretty, flirtatious young girl, and soon Rachile meets Victor. At that time, in that world, degrees of separation were no more than two. Victor was Noach's cousin. Noach, I remind you, had first been in love with my mother's best friend, Rose. However, since Rose's heart was already engaged by Albert, Noach asked Rachile for a date. *She* was not one to be satisfied with being second-best.

"Why not Frieda?" Rachile said.

As it turned out this was a very good suggestion. Noach and Frieda lived pretty happily ever after.

With Victor it was another matter. He was handsome, *truly* handsome; not very tall, but a real charmer, with thick, wavy black hair and a way with women: women threw themselves at him. *Women?* Girls. Victor was Rachile's age, barely out of his teens. But girls threw themselves at him. He'd had dozens of girls.

"I love you," said Victor to Rachile in the course of things.

"Liar!" she reproached him.

He wrote her a letter: "I think about you all the time. I can't sleep."

That did it. They got married in 1926.

—

In our house, where a photograph of Lenin hung on the attic wall (I used to think it was my grandfather) and people were always rushing around to Party meetings, anyone with ambition to be holier-than-thou—and Rachile was nothing if not competitive—had her work cut out for her. In 1931, she made a pilgrimage to the Revolution. It happened that she went by herself; Victor, being a milliner—a seasonal trade— was working his season. I'm not sure how many places in the Soviet Union Rachile visited, but I know she was in Odessa. If, in Odessa, she heard some talk about the forced collectivization of the peasantry and its unpleasant consequences, no doubt she dismissed it: You-can't-make-an-omelette-without-breaking-eggs, can you? Didn't the Soviet Union have to modernize, industrialize, overcome centuries of feudalism, and quickly? How else could the five-year plan be realized? And, anyway, how bad could things be? You could still get food in Odessa.

Moreover, a lot of Rachile's attention was taken up with Victor's brother, Misha. (Just how close their friendship became, I can only guess from Rachile's coy references in later years, and from the picture of Misha she showed me; he was even handsomer than Victor, if you can believe it.)

Whatever happened in 1931—it was a short trip—Rachile came home with news of the miraculous Revolution. *Everybody* in the Soviet Union was happy, *everybody* was excited, *everybody* was involved in creating the new Soviet man. Under Stalin's leadership, guided by Marxist-Leninist thought, a new world was being born. She and Victor would have to work very hard, but they *must* be part of this wonderful experiment. Not to mention that the Depression was raging and the final collapse of capitalism was at hand. Therefore, they'd better get on the stick.

So in 1932, off go my aunt and uncle into history's maw, which happens to be a kolkhoz in Ukraine. Of course this was the very moment when Stalin's campaign of terror, his policy of starving this troublesome area to death, was reaching its apogee. This time Rachile noticed.

If my aunt Rachile were alive today, I'd tell her a riddle I recently heard:

Q: *How do we know that Marxism is a theory, not science?*

I don't know, darling. How?

A: *If it were science, they'd have tried it on dogs first.*

I know my aunt; she'd have had the last word: "They did try it on dogs. On cows. On horses. You think the animals had it any better?"

—

Rachile and Victor managed to get out of the Soviet Union about a year later. They came home having seen what they saw and knowing what they knew. Rachile, as you can imagine, was not one to keep her mouth shut. Of course she should have known that you cannot talk to people who have a lock on truth—hadn't she herself been one of them? Of course she would be ignored and reviled! Marx and Lenin, even forgetting about Stalin, balanced against *Rachile?* What did *Rachile* know? *She* had no firm political grounding, *she* never studied Marxist theory; *she* was a bourgeoise, accustomed to the soft life, exaggerating everything as usual, to make herself important. She was always a troublemaker. And, anyway, even if there *was* something in it, she was weak; you had to be like *iron* to be a revolutionary; you can't make an omelette without breaking a few eggs, isn't that so?

—

Rachile was barely thirty when she and Victor got back to America. Her sisters and brothers were having children. Oscar had a little girl; Joe had one too. Lily, that mean bitch—yes, *bitch*—was barren, which showed there was at least some justice in the world; Bella had had a miscarriage but was trying again.

Rachile loved Frieda, hated Lily. Sometimes she loved Bella, sometimes hated her; not hated, really. Personally, I think she worshipped her but was kept at a distance. Bella was Rachile's touchstone. Role model, as they say these days.

"You know, Dotsicle," Rachile said to me once. "Everyone admired your mother. She had a wonderful mind, not just clever."

—

When Bella gave birth, Rachile was just four months behind her. Each sister had an adorable little girl. See how many pictures of them were taken by their proud parents! Two tiny girls together in a playpen; on the lap of one father or the other; gazed at adoringly by one mother or the other; on a homemade swing, shamelessly, sweetly naked; barely standing, with their baby arms around each other's shoulders. I think Rachile believed that her child would level the playing field, be her buffer, a liaison to the family; change her status from scapegoat into a woman among women, sister among sisters. The past would fall away.

—

"My sisters ruined my marriage," Rachile told one and all. What did she mean by that? That Victor had affairs with her sisters, serially? I don't think so. Maybe Victor did have affairs, but, according to Rachile, so did she. I think she meant that her sisters took Victor's side.

Miserable creature! Selfish beast! These words followed in her wake like poisonous insects. Victor was heard to remonstrate: "What's the matter with you? None of your sisters got a better husband! They say so, too."

—

But what did I know about all this? I was all warm and cozy in my aunt's love.

"You know, Dotsicle, your mother was always going to meetings. She would leave you with me. They put you in the attic to sleep, and it was so hot up there, you'd cry and cry.

I'd take you out on the roof and walk back and forth with you. I adored you. I loved you so much."

With her own daughter, she didn't do so well. *"Selfish! Miserable creature!"* she screamed at little Vivian.

———

Rachile undertook my education along with her daughter's.

"Girls," said Rachile one day when she picked us up after kindergarten. "Girls, what would you do if a man offers you candy and wants to take you for a ride in his car?"

We looked blank.

"You say *no!* You understand? You tell him, 'My mother said I can't go with you.' "

She left us and went around the corner. A minute later, an old man approached us. "Girls," he said. "Want some candy?"

Vivian and I looked at each other. Candy? She didn't say we couldn't have candy. She said we couldn't have candy *and* go for a ride in a car. I think we already had the candy in our mouths when Rachile came rushing back from her surveillance post around the corner.

"Girls," Rachile said some years later. "What would you do if you were getting undressed and a boy came into the room?"

We were dumb.

"Never be ashamed of your body!" said my aunt Rachile.

"Don't rush to cover yourself up. Be proud." (She herself was very proud. If she happened to be naked when the doorbell rang, she never rushed to cover herself up. *Au contraire.*)

"Girls," Rachile said some years after that. "I have a surprise. I'm taking you to the theater." She took us to see *Darkness at Noon*.

There was a gauntlet thrown down at my mother's feet.

—

As the years went by, Rachile's relations with the rest of the family somehow worsened. Now the focus was money. She got involved in a real estate deal with my father; he promised her big profits. She lost most of the investment and complained bitterly that the *scoundrel* had cheated her (and maybe he did). She claimed that Lily was as mean to Vivian as she had been to Rachile, and that Lily's money was going to Bella's daughter, *nothing* for Vivian. (There was something in that.) She told people that Bella and Lily had conspired to get Oscar's money in their own names, ostensibly so that his first wife couldn't get at it but, really, to keep it for themselves. (I doubt that one.) Even her twin brother, Joe, denied her a loan when she asked for it. Poor Rachile. As happens to bitter, loquacious people, confidants become like hens' teeth.

Rachile and Victor retired to Santa Monica. Victor died there, suddenly, of a heart attack. Soon after that, Rachile moved north, to Oakland, to be close to Vivian. She lived in a retirement home. Her physical health was good, but she was plagued by depression; again and again she said she wanted to die. During those last years I spoke to her by telephone, and saw her a few times. Once, Vivian took her to Florida. I met them there and we all stayed with Bobby, Frieda's daughter.

"You know, Dotsicle," Rachile told me then. "Your mother very much wanted another child after you were born."

"Really?" I said. News to me.

"Yes. But she could never get pregnant again. She used to say to me, 'When we go, Dotsy will be all alone. She'll have no one.' "

—

The very last time I spoke to my aunt Rachile, she was in the hospital.

"How are you, Tante darling?" Did she know who I was?

"Terrible, terrible, Dotsinka."

"Tell me what hurts you."

"That mother I got," she said. "You know the one. I don't feel she gave birth to me. She's like a stranger."

NIGHT FALLS ON

TRANSYLVANIA

—

So. I was grief-stricken. Who would have thought? I'd complained so *bitterly,* and they'd been so *old*; I'd been on a death-watch for *so* long. Grief took me by surprise. Would you believe, for instance, that while standing on line in the supermarket I'd be engulfed by a memory so overwhelming that I'd hear myself moaning aloud?

When something like that happens in a public place, it's best to be nicely dressed.

———

You know, my mother had high hopes of my father's retirement years. Mostly she hoped they would travel. Many of her friends went on tours to China with their husbands, they had adventures at elder hostels, they went to Florida every winter. But Mama couldn't get my father to budge (oh, no! Daddy had business; he had to sit on the porch handing out money to lowlifes); and the older she got the less she wanted to part from him. So you could count the travels of her life on the fingers of one hand: a few trips to Florida to visit her sister Lily; a trip to California to see her cousin Meyer; a bonus visit to St. Louis to see her brother Joe just because the cross-country bus stopped there on the way back from California. And then, in the early seventies, she decided to go home to what was still Soviet Russia. She asked me to come with her.

"Why doesn't Daddy go?" I said, knowing Daddy.

"You know Daddy," she said.

Of *course* I could have gone. Why *didn't* I? And why did I never ask her a simple question?

What was it like where you were born, Mama? Was the countryside beautiful? Did you see mountains? hills? a

river? Was the snow very deep in winter? Did you pick
berries in the spring?

The truth is that even if I'd asked, Mama wouldn't have
been much help. When it came to the natural world, she
tended to be a little high-handed, Marxist even; something
on the order of nature simply being an instrument in the
course of human progress. "It was nice," she might have
said. Or, "It wasn't so nice." Or, "It was the way it was.
Snow? Berries? Sure, we had them."

—

When my mother and father were five years dead, I found
myself in Romania, traveling around Transylvania with my
friend Sylvia. We saw breathtaking things. We saw time im-
memorial. We saw landscapes as beautiful as a fairy tale, all
green, folded hills and silver rivers. We saw people in the po-
etic postures of backbreaking labor. We were hounded by
Gypsies. We saw women harnessed to plows, and men carrying donkey-burdens on their backs. We saw animals beaten,
and a shepherd kissing his pretty lamb on the mouth. We
saw women spinning yarn by the roadside. We drank instant
coffee mixed with Coca-Cola, because there was no water. We
squatted over foul latrines. We saw children sickened by the
downwind from Chernobyl. We saw the traces of beautiful
ancient cities hideously remade by actually existing Com-

munism. We climbed a mountain with a hundred thousand religious pilgrims. We saw Jews from America trying to find traces of families lost in Romania's Holocaust. We saw the Museum of Totalitarianism, and outside, we met an old man who had spent forty-one years in Siberia. We were housed and fed by virtual strangers.

On an evening in early June, we drove to see friends of Sylvia's at their dacha, just outside a city called Miercurea-Ciuc. A rutted dirt road led to a few little houses, each with its own garden, clustered at the bottom of a high green hill. We made toasts and drank schnapps. We went to the house next door, where our host's sister lived with her family, drank more schnapps, made more toasts. Stories were told in Hungarian. We laughed. I told stories in English. We laughed. We ate little meatballs and bread with mustard, and drank some more. A sudden rainstorm rolled over the hill. When it had passed we climbed the hill to the summit, up to rolling meadows covered with wildflowers.

The evening glowed with the clear, golden light of summer twilight after rain. The sound of cowbells broke the stillness, and a procession of a hundred cows majestically crested the hill. Two dogs dashed in ecstatic circles. The thirteen-year-old daughter of the family ran ahead, perfectly, heartbreakingly beautiful in this moment of her life.

It had been dusk, only a few nights before, when I stood at the edge of the Tisza River looking across at Ukraine. I wasn't quite there, but I was as close as I was ever going to get. And now, in this odd and wracked corner of the world, on this hill, in the midst of this family I had never seen before and never would again, grief slipped away. I felt happy as the day is long. Maybe it was the schnapps. Night fell.

ACKNOWLEDGMENTS

I am surely debt-ridden: in a literary way, especially to the late Sergei Dovlatov, for his small (in length) masterpiece, "Ours." For inspiriting words, to say nothing of generous deeds, I owe more than I can say to Richard Poirer, Michael Train, Richard Howard, Craig Raine, Elsa and Norman Rush, Kitty Ross, David Alexander, Lucretia Stewart, Vivian Mazur, Barbara Levoy, Jenny Snider, Leah Gardner, Ed and Nancy Sorel, Anna Hamburger, Helene Pleasants, the late Jean Evans, George and Edith Penty, John Bowers, Sylvia Plachy. Many thanks to my agent, Georges Borchardt. To Dan Menaker, writer, editor, dear old friend: if it's not too embarrassing, a kiss. And to Ben Sonnenberg, always my first reader, always first with his two cents, deep and loving gratitude from his cranky wife.

———

These stories are drawn from the once-upon-a-time in the common life of my family when we clustered as closely as bees in a hive. Now we are scattered and few. My cousins have their own stories, which would surely be otherwise. I hope they will indulge me in mine.

DOROTHY GALLAGHER was born and raised in New
York City, where she lives with her husband, the writer
and editor Ben Sonnenberg. She is the author of *Hannah's Daughters* and *All the Right Enemies: The
Life and Murder of Carlo Tresca*.

ABOUT THE TYPE

This book was set in Bodoni, a typeface designed by Giambattista Bodoni (1740–1813), the renowned Italian printer and type designer. Bodoni originally based his letterforms on those of the Frenchman Fournier, and created his type to have beautiful contrasts between light and dark.